Teaching and Learning
in a Microelectronic Age

by
Harold G. Shane

A Publication of the Phi Delta Kappa Educational Foundation
Bloomington, Indiana

Cover design by Peg Caudell

Library of Congress Catalog Card Number 86-63343
ISBN 0-87367-434-0

Dedication

Once again, for Kate,
my very dear wife
and helpmate.

Table of Contents

Part Two: Confronting New Realities in Education

Foreword

One of the major phenomena of the past four decades has been the way in which microtechnologies have penetrated our society. The home, school, workplace — virtually all dimensions of life have been profoundly influenced. Educators in particular have had their profession mediated by the computer, which has become in many ways a paraprofessional partner.

One of the problems generated by the speed and sweep of change associated with the microchip is the task of keeping informed as teachers and as citizens. For this reason, Phi Delta Kappa is pleased to publish *Teaching and Learning in a Microelectronic Age*, a source of general background information with implications for educators. This volume is an elaboration of two widely reprinted *Phi Delta Kappan* articles, "The Silicon Age and Education" (January 1982) and "The Silicon Age II: Living and Learning in an Information Epoch" (October 1983).

This publication is the third monograph on futures studies written by Harold G. Shane and published by Phi Delta Kappa. The earlier monographs were *The Educational Significance of the Future* (1973) and the Phi Delta Kappa Diamond Jubilee volume, *Educating for a New Millennium* (1981).

Dr. Shane, University Professor of Education at Indiana University, is one of Phi Delta Kappa's most widely published authors, having written approximately 60 articles and books for us in the past 30 years. It is fitting, on the publication of this volume, to express Phi Delta Kappa's appreciation to Dr. Shane for his scholarly productivity, which we have been privileged to share with our members and the wider education community over these many years.

Lowell C. Rose
Executive Secretary
Phi Delta Kappa

Acknowledgements

I would like to acknowledge both my gratitude and my sense of debt to those scholarly, informed friends and colleagues who offered guidance and provided information during the two years of research that were invested in *Teaching and Learning in a Microelectronic Age* prior to writing the manuscript in the autumn and winter, 1985-86.

During the early stages of my inquiry into the penetration of education by microelectronics, I was fortunate to have interviews with Margaret Sutton, senior staff member of *Encyclopaedia Britannica;* William Nault, president of *World Book;* and Helen Wright of the American Library Association.

During two months of data gathering in Great Britain, Lord Walter Perry of Walton, long-time head of the British Open University, and a number of his senior staff helped me to understand the changing status of "distance learning" based on electronic instructional materials. Also generous with their time were William Taylor, former chief officer at the University of London (now rector at Hull University), and his colleague Brian Holmes, head of Comparative Education.

Peter Wilby, education writer for the *London Times,* gave me useful information on current and probable developments of computer use in British schools. William Gray of the Strathclyde Education Authority in Glasgow was helpful with information on the changing scene in Scottish schools. Also, Ivor K. Davies, a valued colleague at Indiana University, merits my appreciation for interviewing a number of British scholars working in the realm of microelectronics.

As in the past, the editorial skill and professional judgment of Derek L. Burleson, editor of Special Publications for Phi Delta Kappa, were indispensable resources. He remains one of the very best among hundreds of editors with whom I have worked, for his ideas and attention to detail and for his forbearance when the complexity of the topic kept me from making initial deadlines. To David Ruetschlin, assistant editor at Phi Delta Kappa, I offer my sincere appreciation for his meticulous handling of the many details involved in the production of this book.

I also owe a debt, one far too vast to acknowledge, to the authors of some 1,400 references consulted between 1983 and 1986. A debt to my research assistants can, however, be warmly acknowledged. They include Julie Jo Mortier, Judy Abrahamson, Rosemary Rehak, and Shelly Contreras, all doctoral students who provided such valuable services as maintaining files, annotating reference cards, scanning the literature for items I had missed, and helping to compile the bibliography at the end of this monograph.

Appreciation also is due Sue Logsdon and Barbara Crowe, project typists, who displayed both skill and patience.

Last of all, and of most importance, was the help and sustaining support of my wife, Catherine McKenzie Shane. A former senior vice president in the editorial division of Encyclopaedia Britannica/Compton's, her advice, editing, patience, and love were of consummate importance.

Harold G. Shane
March 1986

Part One

Some Implications of the Computer, Microtechnologies, Robotics, and Global TV for Education

Everything that can be invented has been invented.
—Charles H. Duell, Director
U.S. Patent Office, 1899

*The radio is a commercial failure and its
popularity with the public is waning.*
—Thomas A. Edison, 1926

Chapter 1
The Microelectronic Milestone

I never think of the future. It comes soon enough.
— Albert Einstein

Humankind has passed a number of milestones. Each resulted in a "system-break" — a profound change in the way people lived thereafter. One milestone was reached when humans began to recognize that they were creatures who could think, who became aware of their existence — of their humanity. Another milestone was the development of agriculture, a system-break that permitted nomadic hunters to become farmers whose lives had greater stability and whose produce permitted the rise of cities in ancient times. The concept of God also led to indelible changes in the ways in which our forebears ordered their lives. The development of writing likewise was a potent creation, promoting access to knowledge.

In the past 600 years major changes have occurred with increasing rapidity. Among them were the Renaissance, which invigorated life and learning in the 14th century; the printing press, which promoted communication and education; and the Industrial Revolution, which replaced human muscle power with machines.

Among recent milestones, each confronting us with increasing speed, were the techniques of "inventing inventions" by means of the scientific method and the birth of the "electric surround" — Marshall McLuhan's phrase to describe the "extensions of man" made possible by such inventions as the radio, TV, hi-fi, motion pictures, typewriter, and telegraph.[1] Illustrating the power and impact of Western technology, McLuhan tells us:

> One example is the Bedouin with his battery radio on board the camel. Submerging natives with floods of concepts for which nothing has prepared them is the normal action of all of our technology.[2]

The Microchip Milestone

McLuhan did not live to experience the human extensions made possible by the microchip milestone and the information society it has fostered — a milestone that is inundating all of us with sensory stimulation for which we had little more preparation than did the Bedouin. Indeed, our microelectronic surround could turn us into homogenized Blondies and Dagwoods unless we quickly begin to think with care and to act with prudence. Thus the major purpose of this volume is to examine how educators can learn to live with the silicon chip so that it proves to be a milestone rather than a millstone, which conceivably could hang around our necks in the 1990s.

The Acceleration of Change

A starting point for coping with and profiting from the microelectronic era is understanding the developments that are occurring with almost incredible speed. Let us look more closely at what appears to be happening. Until the world moved into the microelectronic era, changes in lifestyles and work took place at a glacial-to-leisurely rate. People died in a world very much like the one into which they were born. Even major system-breaks did not create rapid changes until the present century. To illustrate, when the last Roman emperor was deposed in 476 A.D., Rome's power, extending from the Mediterranean to Hadrian's Wall, came to an end. But despite its historical significance as a system-break, the fall of Rome did not create profound differences in the way people lived during the Dark Ages that followed. Soldiers still confronted one another with bow and arrow, shield, sword, and spear. Horses pulled wagons or carriages; crops were raised and cattle were herded in the same old ways.

As late as 1920, if George Washington could have been transported from the 1700s to a Midwestern farm in the United States, there would have been relatively little that had happened in the 150-year interval to bewilder him. Horses still pulled carts, oil lamps and candles continued to illumine many homes, and harvesting on most farms continued to be based on human and equine muscle power. It is true that radios, the automobile, aircraft, and electric lights had made their debut, but their impact on the lives of most Americans was just beginning to make itself felt.

It is in the past 60 years, as biophysicist John Platt points out, that "the convergence of today's technological forces has produced a roaring waterfall of change."[3] Nuclear power and weaponry have appeared. The space capsule "Pioneer" has zoomed toward distant Pluto and is headed for the outer reaches of the universe. Artificial life forms have been created. Moon landings and planetary probes have taken place. The "pill" has given women reproductive freedom. Jet planes span continents in four hours. Mammals recently have been cloned. In-vitro conceptions, in-the-womb surgery, and major organ transplants are now becoming routine. And marvels have been accomplished in the realms of "designer genes," holography, and in the divers uses of laser beams in industry and communications.

So rapidly have innovations burst upon us that we are moving beyond what Alvin Toffler labeled "future shock" into a state of hyperturbulence, which Selsky and McCann define as "the condition that results when available resources and institutions prove inadequate to deal with the speed and diversity of change."[4] Daily reports in the media abound with examples of hyperturbulence: astronomical fiscal deficits, nuclear accidents, environmental pollution, widespread world hunger, international terrorism, drug abuse, and other horrors in which our age specializes.

The acceleration of change has made the world of the 1980s significantly different from that of the 1920s. However, it is *changes in the nature of change* that have made the microelectronic milestone unique. For the first time we are confronted by incredible and unexpected technological input, which constitutes a system-break that has dramatically altered our lives.

Overview

In *Teaching and Learning in a Microelectronic Age* I shall explore how and why many of the guidelines that governed our lives in the past have been swept away or altered by contemporary high-tech developments, with attention in later chapters directed to some of the educational implications of these changes in the home and workplace.

Chapter 2 reviews some of the past and current developments in microelectronics and probes a few of the ways in which the microchip is permeating society, creating problems and opportunities both in the workplace and the home. The educational and industrial impacts of the computer and its peripheral equipment are explored in Chapter 3, with particular attention to the use of computers in educational institutions and in an information society. Chapter 4 treats developments in the use of robotics, which a number of schools are exploring. As of 1985 the computer-brained robot is being used in more than 2,000 schools and 1,200 colleges.

In Chapter 5 attention is given to the mixed blessing of the media. Here I document the growing power of TV and discuss the importance of educating young learners so they can cope with the sex and violence frequently depicted and with bias in selected news telecasts and various publications.

5

Part II examines some of the issues and opportunities of the silicon chip era. Chapter 6 sums up the issues that microtechnologies have created in the years since the first computer made its debut in 1946. Attention is given to prudent educational policies mandated by the growing impact of our microelectronic milieu. In Chapter 7, I argue that current reform movements such as *A Nation at Risk* do not give sufficient heed to the influence of high-tech developments. *Redesign* of U.S. education is advocated rather than "band-aid" *reforms* aimed at improving yesterday's schools. The concluding chapter presents the need to make curriculum content more congruent with the microelectronic age we have entered. Changes at all levels from early childhood education to programs for mature learners are considered.

For reference purposes, a selected bibliography and summaries of some major reform reports are included.

Footnotes

1. For a prescient preview of the impact of "electric surround," see McLuhan's *Understanding Media: The Extensions of Man* (New York: McGraw-Hill Paperbacks, 1964).
2. Ibid., p. 16.
3. John Platt, "The Acceleration of Evolution," *The Futurist* (February 1981): 23.
4. John W. Selsky and Joseph E. McCann, "Social Triage: An Emergent Response to Hyperturbulence," *World Future Society Bulletin* 18 (May-June 1984): 1-19.

Chapter 2
The Micro Milieu: Backgrounds, Foregrounds, and Changing Lifestyles

> *"The millennium is at hand. Man has invented everything that can be invented. He has done all he can do."*
> *These words were spoken by a bishop at a church gathering in 1870. They were challenged by the presiding officer, who said that man would one day devise a machine in which to fly.*
> *"Blasphemy!" the bishop cried, "Flight is reserved for the angels."*
> *The bishop was Milton Wright, father of Wilbur and Orville Wright who, years later, developed the first successful flying machine.*[1]

As the above anecdote suggests, it is unwise to underestimate human ingenuity. Since early times humans have devised machines to replace muscle power and reduce physical toil. Less recognized are the efforts we have made to enhance or to extend the power of our minds. In ancient Rome, for instance, colored stones were used to facilitate calculating. The ancient abacus was a similar device but vastly more sophisticated. It was so successful that it still is used in Asia alongside electronic calculators.

Now the microchip is extending our mental powers. The microelectronic developments of recent decades are having a profound influence on the ways in which we order our lives. Changes are occurring with such speed it is difficult to envision what is likely to take place in the short-term future — the next 15 to 20 years. As for the long-term developments — those that will take place in the next millennium, in which today's young learners will spend most of their lives — we can only speculate as to what microtechnologies will accomplish in medicine, industry, education, agriculture, and other realms.

Backgrounds of the Microelectronic Era

Let us look briefly at the sequence of impressive developments and innovations that are leading us from current marvels toward such phenomena as fifth-generation computers possessing artificial intelligence, beginning with the developments that enabled humans to weave numbers by using machines.[2]

Early beginnings. The progenitor of machines that perform arithmetical functions was devised by the brilliant 17th-century French mathematician, Blaise Pascal. One could dial numbers on Pascal's addition-subtraction calculator, and the wheels and cogs inside aligned themselves to show the sum or difference displayed in a small window. Another genius in the realms of philosophy and mathematics born shortly after Pascal in 1646 was Gottfried Wilhelm von Liebnitz. He modified Pascal's calculator so it could handle multiplication and division problems. For more than 300 years the mechanisms developed by Pascal and Liebnitz were the basis for the design and construction of calculating machines.

Charles Babbage, a distinguished British engineer born in 1791, created a mechanical calculator technology that was capable of processing information in a manner not unlike that of modern computers. At the time he worked in the mid-19th century, technology was not sufficiently sophisticated to implement his remarkable insights. Babbage was assisted in his work by a gifted mathematician, Ada, Countess of Lovelace and daughter of Lord Byron. The Countess is credited with devising the concept of programming used in Babbage's calculator.

Contemporary Phases of Computer Development

Phase one: ENIAC makes its debut. The first phase of contemporary electronic computers began with the development of ENIAC at the Moore School of Engineering, University of Pennsylvania. ENIAC, the acronym for Electronic Numerical Integrator and Calculator, was funded by the U.S. government during World War II. Its original purpose was to reduce the time and the tedium involved in calculating the trajectories of artillery shells.

The specifications for ENIAC, which began operation in 1946, are impressive. It required floor space equivalent to a small gymnasium, used 18,000 made-to-order vacuum tubes, and took 130,000 watts to operate. It weighed 30 tons and cost half a million dollars − a considerable sum in 1946.

Ironically, ENIAC was obsolete almost as soon as it was completed because the Bell Labs, in 1947, developed the transistor. Parts of ENIAC remain at the University of Pennsylvania today. Nearby hangs a sign that reads: "In less than 40 years, advances in microelectronics technology have enabled the digital computer with performance far superior to ENIAC to be placed on a one-quarter-inch piece of silicon."

Phase two: The transistor and microchip appear. The transistor combines electrical circuits in a much more tiny space than vacuum tubes and uses semiconductor materials such as silicon, which are less costly than vacuum tubes — an attribute that hastened its acceptance. A few years later, in 1959, single chips with several integrated electronic circuits were devised.

The microchip, which was to make even greater and more rapid developments occur in the home and in the workplace, was introduced in 1970. The chip, no larger than a child's little fingernail, contains thousands of integrated circuits. By the 1980s more than 100,000 transistors could be integrated on a single microchip. It staggers the imagination to realize that each of these tiny silicon wonders had a computing power equivalent to the 30-ton ENIAC with its 18,000 vacuum tubes.

The trend toward electronic hyperminiaturization is continuing with no end in sight. Experimental work by Kenneth Hanck and Keith DeArmond at North Carolina State University in the mid-1980s involves efforts to replace microchips with imprinted molecules that occupy one-millionth of the space the chip requires. Cornell University has a project under way to etch salt crystals with words 10 nanometers high. If the work is successful, the entire contents of the *Encyclopaedia Britannica* could be compressed to fit a piece of software about the size of a postage stamp.

Foregrounds of the Micro Revolution

The current scene: toward a fourth-generation computer. By 1985 the memory of the microchip was in the process of being increased tenfold by VLSI (Very Large Scale Integration); and its memory capacity is maintained — unlike in earlier chips — when power flow is interrupted.

Another development in microtechnology of even greater promise getting under way in the late 1980s is a shift to the use of laser beams in lieu of electric current. The novel feature of this development involves the replacement of transistors with transphasors, devised by Desmond Smith at Heriot-Watt University in Scotland. The transphasor not only performs the same function as the transistor but does so several hundred times faster by using the laser beam.

Of especial importance to the fourth-generation optical computer, in addition to its increased speed and versatility, is that programming is not limited to binary arithmetic; and various computer functions can be carried out at

9

the same time. Since knowledge in the 1990s, according to Daniel Bell, will be doubling every 24 months if present trends continue, the fourth-generation computer, by good fortune, promises to make its appearance just in time to help us cope with the enormous build-up of information.

Public acceptance of computers is reflected by the fact that in 1976, when the electronic cottage was just beginning to move beyond the novelty stage, there were 400,000 in our homes and offices. Ten years later there were six million installations. Shurkin estimates that half of U.S. households will acquire computer systems by the early 1990s.[3] In view of these statistics, the "electronic surround," which Marshall McLuhan foresaw with great pre-science more than 20 years ago, has become a reality. Actually, it is now a *microelectronic* surround as computers and robots permeate homes, banks, farms, offices — touching almost every aspect of our lives.

Toward a fifth generation of "thinking computers." The first four genera-tions of computers reflect the remarkable human ingenuity that carried us from vacuum tubes to transistors to microchips to superchips in less than 40 years. But perhaps the most remarkable development, with enormous implications for teaching and learning in a microelectronic age, is current efforts to produce in the next 10 to 15 years a computer that performs some of the functions of our brains — a mechanism capable of thinking for itself.

By 1985 government-supported programs were under way in Japan, com-peting with similar efforts in the United States and Europe, to create a fifth-generation computer with artificial intelligence (AI).[4] As computers that think through and analyze their assignments are perfected, they are likely to assume enlarged roles in government, industry, and education. It is predicted that AI computers eventually will be able to converse with their operators and perform many routine chores (housekeeping, security, etc.) as more intelligent and mobile robots are devised.

An important step on the route to artificial intelligence had been taken by early 1985 when automatic speech recognition was introduced, which enabled computers to respond to the spoken word. A computer-driven con-veyor belt at O'Hare Airport in Chicago sorted luggage in response to bag-gage handlers' verbal orders; voice-activated doorlocks were in the experimental stage in automobile plants; and "Kurzweil Applied Intelligence" in Waltham, Massachusetts, was testing a typewriter that responded to 10,000 spoken words.[5]

Microtech progress as a two-edged sword. While we can marvel at the changes in lifestyles that microelectronic technologies have brought, it is important for readers to be aware of both their bright and dark sides, be-cause there are two dimensions to technological progress. Undoubtedly,

10

many of the sweeping changes in home, health care, school, and work-place will be beneficial. On the other hand, crime, fraud, invasion of privacy, threats to national security, and the need to make constant adjustments and to resolve value conflicts promise to be problems. As Emery Castle phrased it in *Information: The Human Resource:*

> [T]he gravest threat concerns those tools and techniques that we use to manage relations with one another, among groups, and especially among nations. Emerging stresses must not destroy some of these institutions without replacing them with others.[6]

Changing Lifestyles in a Microelectronic Age

Speculations about the future have proliferated since H.G. Wells blended futurology and fiction at the turn of this century. Perhaps the greatest flood of conjectures about tomorrow's world dates from the 1940s when George Orwell wrote *1984* on the isolated isle of Jura in the Inner Hebrides.

Probably the greatest acceleration in forecasting in our electronic era was triggered by the highly controversial Club of Rome report, *The Limits to Growth* (1973). While carefully pointing out that global equilibrium does not mean stagnation, the report stressed the worsening predicament of hu-mankind in such areas as population growth, pollution, dwindling resources, energy depletion, and decline in agricultural productivity in certain parts of the world. The equally doomsday-oriented *Global 2000 Report,* prepared for President Carter by the CIA, the Department of Agriculture, and 11 other federal agencies, depicts a crowded world population of nearly 6½ billion, global malnutrition, acid rain, and other environmental horrors.[7]

On a more positive side, there also has been an outpouring of books since the 1970s emphasizing a brighter future for the world's billions. Herman Kahn and Julian Simon, for example, wrote *The Resourceful Earth* in the early 1980s using the gloomy *Global 2000 Report* data but coming out with almost exactly opposite conclusions. The Golden Anniversary issue of *U.S. News and World Report*, "What the Next 50 Years Will Bring" (9 May 1983) also glows with optimism, as do Tor Ragnar Gerholm and Herman Kahn's *What About the Future*[8] and a survey of scholarly opinions conducted at Arizona State University in 1985 as part of the university's 100th anniver-sary celebration.[9] For educators, a particularly interesting and readable book by Herbert I. London, *Why Are They Lying to Our Children?* (1984) deftly depicts the schism between doomsayers and optimists. Based on a review of more than 50 schoolbooks from major publishers, London con-cludes that:

11

A tidal wave of pessimism has swept across the country, leaving in its wake grief, despair, immobility and paralysis. Gresham's law of education today seems to be that bad news — even when false — will drive good news out of circulation.[10]

In the speculations that follow, I shall examine two major areas permeated by microelectronics: the workplace and the home. I have made an effort to follow a middle path, to align the emerging changes with neither the alarmists nor the advocates of the bountiful future. My focus is on what will happen to people's lives because of the technologies that are developing.

Possibilities in the changing workplace. From a social and an educational perspective, the world of work has begun to change in many subtle ways. Offices and classrooms are assuming a new look as electronic gear is installed. Managerial and administrative roles are changing as yesterday's boss becomes today's facilitator or expediter. Duties are delegated more frequently, and employees more often are encouraged to show initiative in seeking solutions to problems that arise. Since the workplace is probed in some depth in Chapter 4 on robotics, only a small sampling of innovations in our changing work environment are reviewed here. The interested reader also will find "Jobs of the Future," the cover story in *U.S. News and World Report* (23 December 1985, pp. 40-48), a useful source of information.

Career shifts. It now seems highly probable that individuals will less often follow a single lifelong career. A century or more ago a cobbler's son and grandson often became cobblers. As the 20th century wanes, careers — even those in the professions — demand retraining or continuing self-education.

Current training and degree programs no longer are adequate to prepare students to compete for a diminishing number of jobs. Rather, the increasing number of opportunities as new fields open up are creating demands on education institutions to redirect their programs to prepare persons to perform in the microelectronic surround.

But the business world is not waiting for the traditional education institutions to meet this demand. A growing cluster of corporations are spending huge sums of money to educate their current and future employees for new careers. *Time* magazine (11 February 1985) reported that corporate annual expenditures for training and education had reached $40 billion — two-thirds of the total college and university annual budgets in the United States! Some $700 million was spent by IBM alone in 1984-85 on four technical institutes; and some corporations were financing advanced degrees in software engineering.

Our education system has come under serious criticism for its failure to prepare students with the needed competencies for the workplace. The Center for Public Resources, in a survey of 200 companies, reported that there were major deficiencies in persons with high school diplomas in reading, writing, listening, speaking, and handling basic science and mathematics problems.[11] Some 75% of the businesses surveyed by CPR indicated that they found it essential to provide classes in remedial education. This need is emphasized by the Carnegie Foundation for the Advancement of Teaching, which reported that nearly eight million American adults were in training programs funded by business.[12]

It seems likely that many types of jobs will be eliminated in the micro milieu; but with opportunities for re-education, new jobs should replace the jobs becoming obsolete.

Telecommuting and flexitime. As of 1986, several hundred companies were experimenting with telecommuting, a term used to describe work performed by persons at home, via computer and at times of their own choosing. "Flexitime" is another term used for time choices employees have in a paperless, computerized office often miles from home.

There are both advantages and some disadvantages in telecommuting. There are no parking problems or commuting expenses. With the cost of computer network equipment becoming more economical, the overhead for companies is manageable. Also, mothers of young children, the physically handicapped, and other employees constrained by circumstances clearly benefit by having an "electronic cottage" as their workplace. On the other hand, lack of social contacts in an isolated environment detracts from the group identity and friendly relationships that are nurtured in a common workplace.

Child care supported by employers. In recent years a large number of women with young children have entered the workplace, partly because of economic necessity but also because of a desire to have a career. Some 65% of American women were employed as of 1985, and at least one-third of them had children aged five or under. One outcome of the shift of women from traditional housekeeping roles to that of wage earners has been the widespread need for day-care centers. A 1984-85 survey indicated that about 3,000 businesses provided centers for preschool-age children of working mothers; but the need far exceeds the supply.

As a long-time proponent of early childhood education, I have mixed emotions about this development. I have long been an advocate of professionally staffed programs for three- to five-year-olds in our public and private schools. Some corporations, to their credit, are providing an essential service, which our education system has long been neglecting.

The high-tech home of tomorrow. While the houses we build for tomorrow may lack some of the charm of times past, they promise to be technological wonders with an enormous potential for home-school relationships. A team of students and professors at the Illinois Institute of Technology recently compiled a list of what they believe is in store for us in tomorrow's habitats.[13] Following is a summary of what homes of tomorrow may have:

- Temperature and humidity controls to monitor exterior weather conditions and adjust thereto — plus solar heating on a wide scale.
- Ductwork and electrical waterlines in "deep floor" networks.
- A robotized food processing center in the kitchen.
- An exercise area equipped with digital recordings of one's blood pressure, pulse, temperature, and the like.
- Computer office/study areas individualized to meet the needs of various members of the family.
- Holographic television with 3-dimensional images that put viewers "in the picture."
- A central voice-directed computer to control other household computers, including a mobile robot to do such household chores as cleaning.
- A forcefield device to detect intruders.

Ray Mason and Lane Jennings offer this sage observation about the house of the future:

> No one can say for certain how long it will take humankind and "housekind" to achieve . . . mutual understanding and cooperation. But the potential is there, and if we human beings once begin to recognize that our buildings and machines can do more *with* us than simply *for* us, the house of the future will not be a slave or a servant but a friend.[14]

Whether the house of the future is "servant" or "friend," there is little question but that massive changes are in the works. Just as electric light bulbs replaced gaslight lamps and just as water under pressure from pumping stations replaced the hand pump in kitchen sinks, so will the contemporary home conveniences such as air conditioning be refined or replaced by things to come.

Videotext and teletext. Probably the most significant microelectronic development in the home with a direct bearing on the work of educators is the array of developments in the videotext and teletext fields.[15]

Videotext (also sometimes called viewdata) is a two-way information system that can be summoned with a computer keyboard. The two-way information flow may be by means of a pushbutton phone, cable-TV systems, or a cable-telephone combination. Teletext is a one-way information service activated by pressing a button or keypad to extract information from the TV signal with which it is intermixed.

On the international scene various names are used for videotext or viewdata. Among them are CEEFAX, Prestel, and Oracle in Great Britain; Antiope in France; and Telidon in Canada. Fiber optics, an innovation involving the use of hair-thin glass fibers to replace more costly and bulky copper wires, will reduce costs and improve efficiency for videotext users. In 1982 alone 14,000 miles of fiber were laid. Chapter 3 discusses networking via home computer in greater depth.

The prospect of the electronically permeated household raises many interesting questions about lifestyles in the coming decades:

- Will we become a stay-at-home society that does its shopping, banking, and corresponding electronically?
- Will the family unit become more tightly knit as a result of living in "electronic cocoons"?
- Will leisure become more home-based as videogames, videocasette recorders, and cable TV find their way into family media centers?
- Will "distance learning" in the home take over as more and more students enroll in electronic colleges and universities?[16]
- Will the home become the center for health and medical care by means of electronic house calls from physicians?
- Will the electronic home be available to only the affluent, thus increasing the gap between the haves and have-nots? Will government programs be needed to provide access to electronic services for the poor and handicapped?

Guidelines for the Future

As this sometimes frightening and always exciting century moves into its final decade, we plan for the future, bearing in mind the wisdom of Ortega y Gasset, who wrote, "Human life is a constant preoccupation with the future." We should strive to create the best of alternative futures in a microelectronic era by keeping in mind the following guidelines for education:

1. Remember that our microkids, the young learners of today, take for granted what earlier generations were incapable of even conceiving.

2. Honor both equality and uniqueness in the forms of educational experiences that our society devises.

3. Engage in curriculum redesign activities that recognize that humans vary enormously; making everything mandatory for all learners is like forcing them to use chopsticks even when they are being served a bowl of soup.

15

4. Promote the concept of lifelong learning, which the world of tomorrow demands.

These guidelines are offered with the hope that they do not reflect Aesop's dictum: "It is easy to recommend impossible remedies."

Footnotes

1. Adapted from "What Man Knows Man's Limitations?" *Phi Delta Kappan* (February 1958): Inside back cover.
2. For a more detailed account of early beginnings summarized here, see Christopher Evans, *The Micro Millennium* (New York: Washington Square Press, 1979), pp. 2-20.
3. J.N. Shurkin, *Engines of the Mind: A History of the Computer* (New York: W.W. Norton, 1984).
4. See Evans, *op. cit.*
5. *Time*, 1 April 1985, p. 83.
6. Emery N. Castle, *Information: The Human Resource* (Washington, D.C.: Resources for the Future, 1981), pp. 9-10.
7. Donella H. Meadows et al., *The Limits to Growth* (London: Earth Island, 1973). U.S. Council on Environmental Quality, *Global Future, Time to Act: Report to the President on Global Resources, Environment and Population* (Washington, D.C.: U.S. Government Printing Office, 1981).
8. Herman Kahn and Julian Simon, *The Resourceful Earth* (New York: Blackwell, 1984). Tor Ragnar Gerholm and Herman Kahn, *What About the Future?* (Stockholm, Sweden: KREAB Development, 1984), (Swedish edition).
9. For a summary, see the Associated Press story, "Future Boosted by Technology," 19 March 1985.
10. Herbert I. London, *Why Are They Lying to Our Children?* (New York: Stein and Day, 1984), p. 34.
11. Reported in *U.S. News and World Report*, 1 April 1985, p. 70.
12. Ibid.
13. Reported by Steve Sanders in the "Tomorrow" section of the *Chicago Tribune*, 24 July 1983, p. 5-1.
14. Ray Mason and Lane Jennings, "The Computer Home: Will Tomorrow's Housing Come Alive?" in *Habitats Tomorrow*, ed. Edward Cornish (Bethesda, Md.: World Future Society, 1984), p. 13.
15. Two excellent sources treating videotext and viewdata are: Shirley Fetherolf, "Telecommunications and the Future," in *Communications and the Future*, ed. Howard F. Didsbury, Jr. (Bethesda, Md.: World Future Society, 1982), pp. 216-222; and John Tydeman, "Videotext: Ushering in the Electronic Household," in *Habitats Tomorrow*, ed. Edward Cornish (Bethesda, Md.: World Future Society, 1984), pp. 16-23.
16. Britain's Open University is the first and the classic exemplar of distance learning. By the mid-1980s the Open University's original reliance on TV was mediated by the computer. In the U.S. during 1984-85, at least seven electronic universities were operating for off-campus learners.

Chapter 3
The Computer: An Educational Partner

. . . remember, please, the law by which we live.
We are not built to comprehend a lie.
We can neither love, nor pity, nor forgive.
If you make a slip in handling us you die!
— Rudyard Kipling
"The Secret of the Machines"

Today Kipling's verses might well be retitled "The Secret of the Computer"! Computers are machines — increasingly intelligent ones — with a growing array of capabilities, but also with a massive cluster of challenges. The point is that the microcomputer is an extension of our minds but also has a capacity for highlighting our shortcomings. It is neither good nor bad. It is what we *do* with it that makes it a helpful partner.

If we use this magnificent new tool with prudence and skill, it promises to help humankind to devise brilliant solutions to many pressing personal-social problems. Used stupidly, this product of our ingenuity could simply hasten our ruin on a threatened planet. Fortunately, the shape of things to come remains negotiable as we move further into the 1990s.

In this chapter I shall examine some of the implications of the microelectronic age for educators with their new microchip partners and a wide range of software and peripheral gear. In addition to microcomputers, teachers are likely to use a corps of "electronic paraprofessionals" that will take learning beyond the confines of the traditional classroom.

The Importance of Holism

In considering the implications of the computer for education, the concept of holism is central. Holism is based on the premise that wholes are greater than the sum of their parts. This concept has long been recognized,

17

particularly in the sciences, where realms of complex inquiry such as physics or chemistry are more than a collection of discrete data. They are interconnected and interdisciplinary systems in which the parts, when they are assembled, give added meaning to the whole.

In educational contexts generated by the increasingly powerful electronic surround, planning must become more deliberately holistic. Educators need to recognize that they can never do any *one* thing in administration, in curriculum planning, or in other aspects of teaching and learning without it affecting other things. It is crucial to understand that anything we do in education (or in the larger society for that matter) most likely will have intended and unintended or unexpected outcomes.

As Isaac Asimov has pointed out:

> The important thing to forecast is not that schools and universities, homes and industries will add . . . microcomputers and satellite telecommunications . . . to their repertoire of instructional techniques. Rather, the crucial question becomes, "What new social inventions will spring from routine usage of these devices to enhance learning?"[1]

Consider for example, the intended and unintended outcomes of the universal availability of television in the United States. When television first came on the marketplace in the late 1940s, the intended outcomes were that it would both educate and entertain. An unintended outcome was that by the 1960s young learners would be spending 16,000 hours watching TV compared to spending 12,000 hours in school! Nor was it expected that more than 600,000 children, on a given evening, would be viewing the late movies between midnight and 2:00 a.m.

Another *unintended* outcome attributed by some to universal TV was the phenomenon of the decline in scholastic aptitude scores. TV was a fixture in most U.S. homes by 1952. Twelve years later, in 1964, score decline began. Significantly, 12 years was the interval needed for a cohort of our TV-saturated youth to move through the elementary and secondary school years.[2]

As educators move ever more deeply into the complexities of the microelectronic maze that has sprung up around us, they should give careful heed to the immediate and intended effects of their policy decisions. But they should give equal heed in their planning to possible *unintended* and *undesirable* outcomes. This is a key point to keep in mind as we examine some of the social and educational implications of the computer.

Our Emerging Electronic Partnership

As we contemplate the emerging role of the computer as an educational tool and as a prospective friendly partner, we find we need new insights

18

and new understandings with regard to the machine-human relationship involved. These new understandings evolve from the area known as "human factors research" or "ergonomics." This area has three major divisions: 1) enhancing the physical comfort of the relationship, 2) making the machine-human interface as "friendly" as possible, and 3) minimizing tensions growing out of the anxiety humans feel when threatened (or think their jobs are threatened) by high-tech developments. Also, when two or more persons are using the computer both as an information and a communication device, machine-human interaction becomes further complicated.

Ergonomics is the science of improving the physical relations between humans and their machines. In the industrial, precomputer era, ergonomics was devoted to reducing human discomfort, stress, and fatigue involved, say, when operating an automobile, a lathe, or a bulldozer. The optimum placement of automobile controls on an instrument panel, for example, is the result of ergonomic studies.

With the advent of computers that require a more intimate association between humans and their machines, the study of ergonomics is being refined and extended to encompass *psycho*ergonomic elements, that is, reducing *psychological* as well as physical distress or strain in the relationship. An example of this is "terminal phobia," the fear some people have when they first sit down at a computer terminal.

Psychoergonomics. In a manner reminiscent of the Luddites,[3] who felt threatened by the new labor-saving machines in British factories in the early 19th century, some workers today may feel uneasy when exposed to robot installations, computerized offices, or computer networking. Likewise in education, we need to be aware that some children, parents, teachers, and other school employees may need help in becoming comfortable with the interaction of mind and machine that the computer imposes.[4]

Another interesting and related phenomenon is that now some four- to six-year-olds have begun to talk to a computer as if it were human. If children talk to their dolls and teddy bears, there seems to be no cause for alarm if they make "pets" of a computer. However, a more serious concern is the intensity of the relationship some adolescents develop with videogames. For example, Daneshmend and Campbell report attacks of artificial epilepsy apparently brought on in young people, both male and female, who played videogames for prolonged periods.[5] Similar findings were reported by Rushton, who described the phenomenon as "electronic space war videogame epilepsy."[6]

This brief discussion of ergonomics and its new psychological dimensions makes clear the sometimes unexpected patterns of our emerging relationship with the computer.

Educational Uses of the Computer

With changes taking place in the micro milieu with such mesmerizing speed, an up-to-date overview is impossible unless done virtually on a day-to-day basis. Therefore, the material that follows is, of necessity, an exercise in compression.

What is computer literacy? One definition of computer literacy is simply mastery of the incredible flood of computer terminology that has expanded (some say eroded) our language: Basic, RAM and ROM, Fortran, byte, bit, hard copy, logo, chip, and software are but a few examples. But computer literacy is more than understanding terminology.

To be computer literate, teachers and students need to understand 1) how computers are influencing life on the entire planet, 2) what roles the silicon chip plays in the storage and retrieval of information, 3) what the computer can and cannot do, 4) a hands-on familiarity with programming, 5) how to evaluate software programs, and 6) the ways in which computer skills are involved in word processing, networking, problem-solving, and the like. As more and more sophisticated generations of computers make their debut, educators should recognize that computer literacy is a continuing process, involving skills acquisition in a lifelong continuum.[7]

Some applications of computers in schools. It is risky to speculate about computer applications in the classroom, because as Sojka has pointed out:

> Advances in science tend to be *autocatalytic;* that is, one conceptual advance or new technique often leads to a whole variety of new approaches . . . [The] process then repeats itself, and the ensuing logarithmic progression results in the production of new information at a rate that would not have seemed possible only a few years before.[8]

Just since the 1970s we have seen the following developments:

1. Burgeoning computer literacy programs for youngsters at all levels that provide a general understanding and appreciation of the applications of computers in school and the wider society.

2. Introduction of drill and practice, simulation, gaming, and self-tutoring computer programs, with continuing efforts to improve and refine software.[9]

3. The use of computers as audiovisual aids as a result of developments in computer graphics.

4. The use of computers for the construction, storage, and scoring of standardized testing materials for assessment of pupil progress.

5. The accessibility of job descriptions and other occupational information for use by counselors in career guidance.

20

6. The replacement of library index cards and library loan records by the computer, which requires staff and students to learn new skills in order to do library research.

7. The use of the computer for long-range planning with respect to school plant, personnel needs, supplies, and curriculum materials.

8. The inservice and preservice education of teachers in such areas as computer skills and evaluation of hardware and software.

9. The use of many types of computer-assisted instruction (CAI) materials providing students with individualized instruction at their own pace.

10. The use of the computer as a record-keeping device, thus significantly reducing teachers' and administrators' busywork in such areas as recording attendance and grades, payrolls, requisitions, form letters, and the like.

11. The use of the computer for the scheduling of classrooms, teacher meetings, laboratories, conferences, and other events.

12. The use of computer information networks, which provide unique opportunities for distance learning and communication. The potential for networking is just beginning to be realized. As of 1985-1986, the Big Three — Source, CompuServe, and Dow-Jones News Retrieval Service — provided nearly 400,000 homes and perhaps a million people with access to teleshopping, newsletters, counseling, teleconferencing, encyclopedia information, and much more through the databases provided.[10] Electronic database information services have grown from 300 worldwide in 1978 to 2,020 as of 1983. Of this number, 1,140 were located in the United States.[11]

Computer applications in school workstations. The sampling of computer applications listed above represent functions performed by a variety of school personnel — from superintendent to transportation director to business manager to testing director, to mention a few. Each represents a workstation for computer use. The number of workstations would, of course, vary among school districts, depending on their size and administrative structure. But it is not difficult to envision the use of computers in practically every aspect of school operations in the near future.

The media services director is an example of a school workstation that already is caught in the deluge of information-glut, which is straining the capacities of our libraries and media centers, especially at the university level. Campbell describes the new technology that seems to be generating a huge "bibliographic utility" comparable to a national telephone system.[12] He also raises many questions as to whether our high-tech know-how is out-distancing our wisdom. Among them is the prospect of inequitable information-handling systems, which could result in impoverished schools and colleges with students in danger of becoming candidates for an "intellectual Third World." Campbell also quotes a distinguished librarian's concern regarding possible information-glut that could leave us "drowning in information and starving for knowledge."[13]

In any case, our workstations are a part of the new electronic partnership between school and computer, and we must learn how to use these new resources.

Beyond the Information Society

Having examined briefly where the information society is moving, attention is now directed toward a more distant future with speculations about new dimensions in tomorrow's microelectronic age.

Alvin Toffler, in his provocative book, *The Third Wave,* conceptualizes historical change in terms of three waves:[14]

1. The agricultural wave, which changed the lives of nomadic hunters as they learned to grow and harvest food crops and later to build the great cities of the ancient world.
2. The industrial revolution, which gradually replaced muscle power with machine power.
3. The information society or third wave, which extended human resources through a succession of microelectronic innovations that provided sources of data and the means of communicating it to others.

Toffler's wave metaphor is helpful in understanding major changes in human history. However, keep in mind that the waves did not succeed one another with precise chronological demarcation points. The agricultural wave was modified by the industrial revolution with its mechanized farming and the introduction of chemical fertilizers and pesticides, so that in the United States one farmer now produces enough food for 50 or more people. The information society wave crested because of inventions made during the industrial era over the past 300 years. And currently, computer-controlled robots have begun to revolutionize factory production. Perhaps a better way of understanding change is viewing the waves as complementary and synergistic.

Growth of the information economy. Since William Shockley invented the transistor in 1947, other technological developments ushering in the information age have been spectacular. By 1956 approximately half of the U.S. labor force was involved in the handling and processing of information. By the mid-1970s the number of farm workers had fallen below 4%, and personnel in industrial or "smokestack" occupations had dwindled to below 20% of the total labor force.

John Naisbitt, in his persuasive best seller, *Megatrends,* suggests that 1956-57 be considered the point at which the "megashift" to the information era occurred.[15] He selects this time period, first, because in 1956 blue-collar workers for the first time were outnumbered by professional, managerial, clerical, and technical workers; and second, 1957 marked the year the Russians launched the Sputnik satellite, which served as a technological catalyst, ushering in a new global era of communications.

One can argue about the date to mark the debut of the microelectronic age, but a good case can be made for the date when the first personal or home computer became available in the early 1970s. By 1981, about three million microcomputers had been sold in the United States. At this writing, during 1985-86, home sales could exceed 60 billion dollars. However, competition for the home computer market is fierce; some manufacturers are cutting back on production because of sales declines and others have gone bankrupt or have gotten out of the business. Nevertheless, the impact of the home computer is undeniable; and the tremendous growth of the information economy is beyond dispute.[16]

A projection of growth in the micro milieu is difficult to forecast because of the new breakthroughs in computer technology, which will have an inevitable impact on the information society. To illustrate, in June 1985 Cray Research of Minneapolis announced the first production model of its $17.6 million Cray II supercomputer. With an internal memory capacity of two billion bytes, this newcomer is 40,000 to 50,000 times faster than a personal computer. A successor to the Cray II, targeted for 1988 production, will operate with even more blinding speed and have an eight-billion byte memory.

Computers with awesome speed, along with divers other functions, are used for such tasks as sorting the huge quantities of surveillance information beamed from spy satellites and ground-based listening posts to U.S. intelligence agencies. It can be reasonably assumed that the advances represented by the Cray II supercomputer undoubtedly will influence trends in the uses and sales of computers on a global basis.[17]

The fourth wave — and beyond? While planet Earth is endeavoring to adjust to the information age or third wave, it is intriguing to ask, Will there be a fourth wave? A fifth? Even a sixth? After examining between 1,200 and 1,400 books and articles that seemed relevant to teaching and learning in a microelectronic age, I am convinced that a fourth wave, while mostly unrecognized in the mid-1980s, is now beginning to surge around

23

us. This is what I call the *microbioelectronic* wave, which is giving us opportunities to process and to apply the flood of data that are being accumulated day by day. Daniel Bell, the distinguished Harvard scholar who wrote with great prescience about the coming of the post-industrial service-society, recently estimated that the rate at which humans accumulate information would double every two years by 1992.[18] This, I contend, is what has brought us to the fourth wave.

I have designated this fourth wave as one that challenges us to assimilate and to use properly this burgeoning source of information. I have chosen the term micro*bio*electronic to define the fourth wave because microelectronic developments are already beginning to impinge on the fields of biology and medicine and are posing difficult decisions of a moral and ethical nature. No consideration of the new computer-human partnership discussed in this chapter would be complete without mentioning these microbioelectronic developments. Let me illustrate my point with a few examples.

- Recently two fertilized ova were "orphaned" by an airplane crash that killed their parents before they could be transplanted to their mother's womb. Did these ova have a right to life with a surrogate mother?

- A woman who cannot conceive now can have another woman's ova fertilized by her husband's sperm and transplanted to her womb, thus, in effect, bearing her husband's child. But is this right or wrong?

- About $1 billion per week is spent in the United States on Medicare. One-third of this money is invested in the terminally ill. Is this deployment of funds desirable?

- An artificial heart, one not approved by the government, was used in an effort to save a man whose body had rejected the human heart used in prior surgery. Was the surgeon's decision appropriate?

- People have offered to sell an organ to hospitals for transplanting, for example, a kidney for $25,000. Is this an acceptable practice?

- Do parents and an obstetrician have the right to let a severely handicapped Baby Doe perish? Or does its right to life prevail?

Other examples can be found in fields other than medicine, such as a cellular life form capable of cleaning up oil spills at sea, which was patented in the late 1970s. The question I raise is: Where do we find the moral, legal, and ethical guidelines to help us cope with the fourth-wave developments, which human ingenuity in using microelectronics is producing?

Beyond the fourth wave. Not only does U.S. education, and the larger society that sustains it, need to recognize the value-oriented issues the fourth wave is presenting, but also we, as educators, need to help a fifth wave to come into being. This might well be a knowledge society built on, but transcending, information per se. The fifth wave thus would be one in which we grapple with the implications of the information and microbiotech waves for a global society. I would hope that, as a knowledge society emerges, a sixth wave also would take form in the coming millennium — a *wisdom society wave* where our schools, families, and social agencies cooperate in helping learners to judge the soundest courses of action from among the many alternatives that the future holds. My vision is an international social order in which humans are learning to make the right decisions — to do the right things — for the right reasons.

Concluding Comment

The microcomputer cannot be considered in isolation. It is an inseparable part of our microelectronic milieu, affecting our schools, families, careers, leisure, social relationships — our very lives. Although the silicon chip is penetrating our schools, our educational planning should be carried forward in the context of the total microelectronic epoch and not confined within the school walls.

In his book, *Experience and Education,* John Dewey offers sound advice about the nature of our responsibility as educators. His words are still timely as we move through and beyond the information society to open up the frontiers of the mind and learn to adapt our lives to the waves that seem likely to follow Toffler's third wave:

> The greater maturity of experience which should belong to the adult as educator puts him in a position to evaluate each experience of the young in a way which the one having the less mature experience cannot do. It is then the business of the educator to see in what direction an experience is heading. There is no point in his being more mature if, instead of using his greater insight to help organize the experience of the less mature, he throws away his insight.[19]

The "greater maturity of experience" Dewey mentions means that we as educators must make a concerted effort to grasp the implications of the micro milieu for all learners. Not to do so would be to throw away those insights in the arenas of teaching and learning, which is our charge.

Footnotes

1. Cited by Christopher Dede, Jim Bowman, and Fred Kiersted, "Communications Technologies and Education," in *Communications and the Future,* ed. Howard F. Didsbury, Jr. (Bethesda, Md.: World Future Society, 1982), p. 174.

2. For an abstract of a CEEB panel report on score decline and the negative influence of TV, see Harold G. Shane, "The Academic Score Decline: Are Facts the Enemy of Truth? An Interview with Willard Wirtz," *Phi Delta Kappan* 59 (October 1977): 83-87, 145, 146.

3. Ned Lud, a simple-minded worker, smashed stocking frames in a textile plant in England and inadvertently launched the early 19th century labor protest movement that bore his name.

4. For data on human factors research, see L.M. Branscomb's prescient overview, "Information: The Ultimate Frontier," *Science* 203 (January 1979): 146-47.

5. T.K. Daneshmend and M.J. Campbell, "Dark Warrior Epilepsy," *British Medical Journal* 284 (12 June 1982): 1751-52.

6. D.N. Rushton, "Space Invader Epilepsy," *Lancet* 1 (1981): 501.

7. Books on computer literacy with classroom applications include: Carin E. Horn and J.L. Poirot, *Computer Literacy: Problem Solving with Computers* (Austin, Texas: Sterling Swife, 1981), and A. Luehrmann and H. Peckham, *Computer Literacy: A Hands-on Approach* (New York: McGraw-Hill, 1983).

8. Gary A. Sojka, "Where Biology Could Take Us," *Business Horizons* (January 1981), p. 60.

9. It is of historical interest to note that in 1926 Sidney L. Pressey of Ohio State University devised a teaching machine that awarded children candy for correct answers. B.F. Skinner also built an early instructional device (1953) for use in arithmetic classes.

10. If one has a touch-tone telephone and a personal computer, all that is needed for networking is a modem (MOdulator-DEModulator to transform acoustical or computer data), software for network interactive participation, and a component that coordinates sending and receiving network data via modem and phone circuit. For readers interested in networking, see Ivor K. Davies and Harold G. Shane, "Educational Implications of Microelectronic Networks," in *Microcomputers and Education,* Eighty-fifth Yearbook of the National Society for the Study of Education, ed. Jack A. Culbertson and Luvern L. Cunningham (Chicago: University of Chicago Press, 1986).

11. James Ducker, "Electronic Information — Impact of the Database," *Futures* 17 (April 1985): pp. 164-69.

12. Colin Campbell, "Torrent of Print Strains the Fabric of Libraries," *New York Times*, 25 February 1985, p. A10.

13. Ibid.

14. Alvin Toffler, *The Third Wave* (New York: William Morrow, 1980).

15. John Naisbitt, *Megatrends* (New York: Warner Books, 1982), p. 12.

16. For a succinct history of the role of the silicon chip, see Colin Covert, "A Brief History of the Indispensible Silicon Chip," *TWA Ambassador* 16 (November 1983): 102-106.

17. For more details on this superpowered machine, see *Time*, 17 June 1985, p. 53.

18. Daniel Bell, cited by Harry L. Freeman, executive vice president of the American Express company, *Vital Speeches of the Day,* 1 July 1986, pp. 572-75.

19. John Dewey, *Experience and Education* (New York: Macmillan, 1938), p. 31.

Chapter 4
The Robot in Industry and Education: Establishing New Relationships

Robots will leave to human beings the tasks that are intrinsically human.
— Isaac Asimov

Of all the microelectronic speculations in print, none were more intriguing during my 28 months of research on the micro milieu than writings on computer-based robotics. Articles and books on the topic range from highly speculative to extremely provocative in their descriptions of the changing fabric of society made possible by robots.

The Robot's Roots

Some background on robots is in order here to provide little-known historical information of sociocultural interest and to set the scene for examining the impact and possible future roles of robotics in education, about which little has been written except for a few prescient books, such as Colin Norman's *The God That Limps*.[1] Therefore, I shall provide an overview of the increasingly important development of computer-controlled robots, which are permeating industry, our homes, and, as we shall see, even our schools.

The robot in myth and history. Fascination with the idea of creating automatons can be found in ancient mythology. According to Greek mythology, Prometheus created the first humans out of clay. Hephaestas, god of metal working and fire, supposedly kept his associates on Mount Olympus happy with technological feats such as robotic serving girls and automated shoes that propelled the gods in their travels.

Turning from mythology to ancient records, we find reports of Archytas or Tarentum (d. 350 B.C.) creating a wooden dove capable of flight. Hero

27

of Alexandria, in his *De Automatis* (200 B.C.), describes a temple in which robots danced. Thomas Aquinas, in the 13th century, allegedly smashed a robot that opened the door in a Dominican monastery in Cologne because he deemed it to be a demonic device. Continuing our brief foray into the past, mention should be made of an automated golem or monster created by Rabbi Judah Loew in 16th century Prague to protect Jews from persecution.

The term "robot" first came into general use when Czech dramatist Karel Capek (1890-1938) presented his satirical play, *R.U.R.*, in 1921. The letters stand for Rossum's Universal Robots. There is some dispute over the meaning of the term in translation. *World Book* (1972 edition) contends that it comes from the Czech word, *robotit,* meaning "to drudge." *Time* magazine (8 December 1980, p. 77) states that "forced labor" is the correct translation; James S. Albus, author of *Brain, Behavior, and Robotics,* agrees but uses the form *robota.*[2] The term "servant" also is used by some writers as the proper translation.

In Capek's play the robots are humanoid in form but engineered to be more efficient than people. They are intended to produce so many goods that humans can obtain everything they need without working – an argument for computerized robots that has resurfaced in the 1980s. The climax of *R.U.R.* comes when Rossum's creations become convinced that they are human, too, and rebel against their oppressors. Perhaps this motivated Isaac Asimov to formulate his Three Laws of Robotics:

1. A robot shall not injure a human being.
2. A robot must obey humans unless their orders conflict with 1.
3. A robot must protect itself as long as its action does not violate 1 or 2.

What Is a Robot?

Although today's robots generally do not resemble people, because of *R.U.R.* and the movie *Star Wars,* with its C3P0 and R2D2 robots, the humanoid image undoubtedly comes to mind. To dispel this fanciful image, let us begin by looking at what a robot is and what it does. Then we shall examine whether robotics could become the "4th R" as curriculum workers plan for the 1990s and the new millennium.

Essentially a robot is a computerized machine that is able to function in a manner similar to a human being. The Robot Institute of America has developed a more elaborate definition:

> A robot is a reprogrammable multifunctional manipulator designed to move materials, parts, tools, or specialized devices through variable programmed motions for the performance of a variety of tasks.[3]

What do robots do? In years past automated devices were developed to perform tedious tasks and to handle heavy objects. For instance, the mechanical loom eased some of the monotony of handweaving, while a steam shovel replaced the muscle power required by a pick and shovel.

As Toren points out, contemporary robots' functions are governed by their three basic components: 1) a body, 2) control mechanism, and 3) power supply. The control begins and terminates the robot's actions, stores data in its memory banks, and interacts with its environment to perform assigned tasks as on an assembly line.[4]

As of 1986, four robot refinements are receiving careful study. These are the power of *vision* and the ability to *hear* instructions, to *speak* through digital recordings, and to have a sense of *touch* through tactile sensors that function like "cat's whisker" feelers for determining the shape and weight of objects.

Enthusiasts such as Joseph F. Engelberger, known as the "father of robotics" and president of Unimation Corporation, see a bright future for automation.[5] His goal, he said in a 1980 interview, was to make robots more like people: "The closer the robot comes to having human flexibility, the more robotic it is."[6]

Brian Toren, a systems engineer with the Sperry Computer System, offers this panegyric of the robot's future:

> Work in artificial intelligence is being used to better understand how a robot can be more finely tuned to perform like a human. Friendly man/machine interfaces are being developed to enable a person, new or recently introduced to programming, to easily and confidently operate this new device.
>
> The future, too, is bright . . . with the robot operating in factories, offices, homes, underwater, and in deep space. The robot will eventually become a servant of humankind which will do all the menial, dangerous, and boring tasks people are presently saddled with and which are often demeaning. With the robot taking over these activities, humankind will be able to get on with the evolution of mind and spirit. The needs met will no longer be physical but spiritual and mental.[7]

The proliferation of robots. The advent of robots — sometimes referred to as the "new industrial revolution" — did not get under way until the late 1960s and early 1970s. The Japanese installed their first Unimation robots in 1967, and in the early 1970s General Motors ordered 50 robotic welding units and by 1980 had acquired about 300. The growth rate since the Seventies has been exponential. Estimates by experts vary because of the way they define various types of automated machines as robots. Nevertheless, the statistics are impressive. Engelberger estimates that 17,000 to 18,000 installations were at work in Japan by 1983. By 1985 the U.S. robot population totaled 7,000 units, and projections made by *U.S. News and World Report* call for between 30,000 and 40,000 units at work in U.S. industries by 1990. Other experts predict that with favorable economic conditions the United States may have as many as 60,000 by 1990.[8]

Wide-ranging applications of robotics. For the past two decades robots have been used primarily on assembly lines of appliance and automobile companies. More recently, we have witnessed many intriguing robotic developments, a sampling of which are listed below:

- An Australian robot that can shear sheep — except for the face and neck.
- A remote-controlled six-wheel device for use in bomb disposal.
- Experiments with a robotized word processor that automatically types oral dictation.
- Surgical techniques developed at Long Beach Memorial Hospital where, by using computerized CAT brain scans, a tiny electrical robot indicates the precise spot where drilling for cranial surgery should be done.
- In a New York City fast-food restaurant, a six-armed robot prepares meals to order, takes money and makes change, clears the table, and sweeps the floor.
- A Japanese automobile robot that can respond to more than 25 spoken commands in any language for which it is programmed.
- According to the *Glasgow Herald*, "Scottish wonder robots" are "giving a great lift to the brewery trade" by loading and unloading 600 beer kegs per hour.
- Development by the Nippon Telegraph and Telephone Public Corporation of a robot that can read with a purported accuracy of 99.5%. The robot's computer has been programmed with a dictionary that, as the robot turns pages, allows the machine to read aloud properly inflected sentences. Such a machine can be used to read to the blind or the illiterate.

A sampling of virtues associated with robots. One of the virtues ascribed to robots is that they will help to erase or reduce the advantage that Japan has enjoyed in recent years — especially in the automotive field. Another is that robots can help control wage inflation. To illustrate, in the 1960s an assembly-line robot cost around $25,000 — a sum that amounted to an hourly cost of $4.20 during the machine's eight-year lifetime.[9] This was comparable to hourly wages and fringe benefits of that era. In the 1980s the price of a typical assembly-line robot was $40,000, and costs to operate it ran about $4.80 per hour. Workers' wages and benefits in U.S. industry often are more than $20 per hour. One can see the obvious economy of robotizing production when one compares a U.S. steelworker's hourly wage of $23.99 including benefits in 1982 to a South Korean's wage of $2.30.[10]

According to Walter K. Weisel, president of the Robotics Industries Association, a shorter work week will result as more and more robots are produced. Also, robots expect no coffee breaks, can work three eight-hour shifts, and eschew any form of sexual harassment.

Because dull, dirty, dangerous, and heavy work can be relegated to robots, workers are willing to accept them as long as industry provides retraining in the technological skills needed to operate and maintain the robots. Since the robots generally are seen as helpers rather than as a threat to jobs, there have been few if any Luddite reactions aimed at sabotaging them. However, labor union officials are likely to be less sanguine if robots pose a major threat to their domains.

Problems associated with increased use of robots. By all odds the greatest concern expressed about the increased use of robots is the potential loss of jobs. In 1984 Weisel concluded that in six years at least 75,000 U.S. factory jobs will disappear, and the prospect of many thousands of new jobs may fail to materialize.[11] Ginzberg is even more pessimistic when he concludes that mechanization and automation is displacing or shifting some two-thirds of our labor force now engaged in producing goods.[12] The unanswered question is: How many new or different jobs will elbow their way to the forefront?

Some innovations already are creating unemployment when, for instance, a factory is retooled and automated. Consider this example:

> The General Electric Company is investing $316 million over the next three years to revitalize its locomotive plant in Erie, Pennsylvania. When all of the robots, computerized machine tools, and other automation systems are in place, the Erie "factory with a future" will have increased its production capacity by one-third.[13]

Obviously, such investments should strengthen the nation's economy by increasing productivity. But the effect on the work force is that two workers will do in 16 hours at General Electric what 70 workers did in 16 days before the plant received its electronic facelift.

According to Vary T. Coates, automation also could become a threat to the future employment of nonwhites and of women. She tells us that lower-level white-collar jobs may be sharply reduced by office automation. She also points out that 16% of our factory jobs are filled by nonwhites and 41% by women. Coates contends that because many of these groups have had little opportunity for formal education, are less likely to be represented by unions, are less mobile because of family ties, and have less job experience, they may suffer the most as we move toward industrial robotics.[14]

Humorist Art Buchwald in a sad/funny column, "The Robots Took Over," comes up with another potential liability in a robotized world. He describes an imaginary visit to a factory making sneakers. Mr. Widget, the owner, laments the fact that this automated production line is making more sneakers than ever before but he can't sell them. Buchwald, in his inimitable way, points out that Widget has saved a fortune in workers' salaries but that the "robots are lousy consumers!" Coates makes the same point:

> Unlike human workers, industrial robots do not buy houses, automobiles or food, they do not pay taxes or draw social security checks. If they are to play a larger part in the future of American industry, it behooves us to think seriously about possible consequences.[15]

It is too early to generalize about the ultimate permeation of our social fabric by various microelectronic devices. But we can be reasonably certain that robots will become increasingly sophisticated and will function with less human supervision, thus mandating the most careful economic and social adjustments. Furthermore, because the people on our planet are becoming so tightly "wired together" by satellites, computers, and robots, both the young and old need a common core of education. Our schools are not yet providing the coping skills that are demanded by the micro milieu. As Maccia points out, "The television tube and computer games have replaced the Roman Arena."[16] The challenge for educators is to help learners gain the insights and ethical judgments needed in the microelectronic age.

Robotics: Some Implications for Education

Acceptance of the robot as a teaching tool is growing. According to Edward Warnshuis, publisher of the journal, *Technological Horizons in Education,* there were at least 2,000 robots in U.S. secondary schools in 1984-85. Also, 1,200 colleges were offering courses in robotics.[17] Further evidence of the interest in robots is "The Robot Exhibit: History, Fantasy, and Reality" created by the American Craft Exhibit in New York, which is on an extended tour of 11 large cities. Also, a number of companies are selling robots designed explicitly for use in schools, colleges, and company training programs. Their colorful names include: TeachMover,

MiniMover, Rhino XR, Genus, Hero I, Oscar, and Topo. Prices range from $1,000 to $15,000. A mail-order catalogue describes Topo as an extension of the home computer. It has a text-to-speech voice synthesizer permitting singing and foreign language use. It is mobile, can serve beverages, and can play games.

Schools in some cities already have robots for use in classes where students are studying electronics. In Orlando, Florida, the police department has acquired "OPD2," a 5'2" robot, which was used in some 400 educational programs in area schools during 1984.[18]

The robot's challenge to education. One of the major challenges presented by robots and other microelectronic innovations is how to avoid preparing students for jobs that are likely to diminish or disappear in the 1990s and thereafter. With the dwindling emphasis on math and science in recent years, our schools have not been geared to produce workers in a high-tech society. There is merit in the proposals of Dale Parnell, president of the American Association of Community and Junior Colleges, who calls for a carefully structured "tech-prep" program beginning in the junior year of high school and extending through the second year of college.[19] It would stress basic skill development in an applied setting to prepare competent technicians needed by the thousands to build, repair, and maintain high technology equipment.

Another challenge facing educators is the impending teacher shortage, already apparent in the fields of science and math. Estimates of the need for additional teachers vary from 200,000 to one million by the 1990s.[20] Without qualified instructional personnel, it is quite possible that electronic means will be used to supplement diminished human resources. As robots acquire increasing versatility, one can envision them serving as "paraprofessionals" in the classroom. Even videogames may have a role in instruction. Long and Long contend that videogames, if properly employed, can become tools for learning.

> Video games clearly possess powerful learning components. Studies indicate that the games are based on the same principles – challenge, fantasy, and curiosity – that motivate learning. The games provide active involvement, the option of quitting when the task goes beyond the learner's ability level, short periods of intense activity, flexible time schedules for learning and a controllable environment. All of these are powerful factors in learning.[21]

Whether as "menace" or "mentor," the robot and other electronic devices present both challenges and opportunities to educators in the coming decades. Joseph Delsen lays out the challenge for us in *Silico Sapiens: The*

Fundamentals and Future of Robots. He states that we must recognize that robotics is comparable in importance to the transistor, and that the field of robotics may prove to be the final step in computer evolution. If we surrender our human prerogative or abdicate our responsibilities, the robot species now evolving could lead to the demise of the kind of humankind our schools are striving to produce.[22]

But as always, human judgment and insight will determine how well we learn to survive in the constantly changing micro milieu. The challenge is to think and to act intelligently. Such qualities do not reside in our machines.

Concluding Comment

Given present trends, it seems likely that our lives will become more and more enmeshed with computers, computer networking, robotics, and the electronic media. There undoubtedly will be problems for a long time to come in such areas as: 1) finding ways for the equitable distribution of microelectronic gear, 2) making the best use of vast information sources accessible by computers, 3) coping with new moral and ethical questions raised by increasingly sophisticated technology, and 4) working out new roles for schools and teachers as we move beyond the era of a fixed curriculum largely limited to finite textbooks.

There is little doubt but that microelectronic wonders will enhance home and other non-school learning experiences. But even with the advent of more versatile and low-cost electronic gear made possible by the silicon chip, it is highly improbable that organized schools, as we know them, will disappear. There are just too many aspects of learning that require human interaction for this to happen. In fact, the efficiency that the computer, robots, and other microelectronic equipment bring to the teaching-learning process could allow more time for the arts and other creative activities in our schools.

Footnotes

1. Colin Norman, *The God That Limps: Science and Technology in the Eighties* (New York: W.W. Norton, 1981).
2. James S. Albus, *Brain, Behavior, and Robotics* (Peterborough, N.H.: Byte Books, 1981).
3. Cited by Brian Toren,"Robot Technology," *Futurics* 6 (1982): 26-34.
4. Ibid., p. 27.
5. Unimation is a subsidy of Westinghouse Electric. Engelberger built his first robot in the early 1960s.
6. Quoted by Fred Reed, "The Robots Are Coming, The Robots Are Coming," *Next* 1 (May/June 1980): 30-37.

7. Brian Toren, op. cit., p. 33.

8. James S. Albus, "Robots in the Workplace," *The Futurist* 17 (1983): 22-27.

9. Otto Friedrich, "The Robot Revolution," *Time*, 8 December 1980, p. 77.

10. Source: World Steel Dynamics, quoted in *Time*, 24 January 1983, p. 58.

11. Quoted in *USA Today*, 3 July 1984.

12. Eli Ginzberg et al., *The Mechanization of Work* (San Francisco: W.H. Freeman, 1982).

13. The June 1983 issue of *The Futurist*, from which this illustration is taken (p. 18), notes that further information can be obtained from the News Bureau, General Electric Company, P.O. Box 5900, Norwalk, CT 06856.

14. Vary T. Coates, "The Potential Impact of Robotics," *The Futurist* 17 (1983): 28-32.

15. Ibid., p. 28.

16. George S. Maccia, "Robotic Learning and Rational Interdependence." Paper presented at the 5th World Congress of Comparative Education, Paris, July 1984.

17. Quoted in "Robots Can Teach While They Serve," *USA Today*, 26 June 1984, p. 30.

18. For additional information, see Sandra M. Long and Winston H. Long, "Robotics: The Fourth 'R'?" *World Future Society Bulletin* 18 (March-April 1984): 15-19.

19. For details see Thomas A. Shannon's article in the *School Board News*, 16 January 1985, p. 3.

20. The National Center for Education Statistics conservatively estimates the need for 200,000 new teachers in 1991. NEA estimates the need for a million by the mid-1990s.

21. Sandra M. Long and Winston H. Long, "Rethinking Video Games," *The Futurist* 18 (December 1984): 35-37.

22. Joseph Delsen, *Silico Sapiens: The Fundamentals and Future of Robots* (New York: Bantam New Age Books, 1986).

Chapter 5
Globalized Media:
Toward Community or Catastrophe?

The most remarkable paradox of our time is that, in proportion as the instruments of communication have increased in number and power, communication has steadily declined. Mutual intelligibility is probably a rarer phenomenon than at any time in history.
— Robert M. Hutchins[1]

The current flood of publications dealing with the deplorable condition of the communications media strongly confirms the late Robert Hutchins' statement, which was written at the threshold of the information society some 30 years ago. As we begin an in-depth look at the current status and role of the media, let us first consider some of the meanings associated with the term, "the media."

There are at least 10 dictionary definitions for the term "medium." The two most appropriate for this chapter are "an intervening thing through which a force acts" and "any means, agency, or instrumentality such as radio, television, or printed materials which serves as a medium of communication." But clearly, computers and the networks built around them, as well as certain types of robots and satellites – indeed, most of the systems that support our microelectronic surround – can be classified as means of communication.

Who are America's media giants? Standard and Poor's Corporation compiled data on the income of the 12 biggest media corporations in 1984 showing revenues totaling more than $25 billion dollars. The table below lists the top 12.

36

Revenues of the 12 U.S. Media Giants (1984)[2]

CBS, Inc.	4.93 billion
ABC	3.71 billion
Time, Inc.	3.07 billion
Times-Mirror Co.	2.80 billion
Dun and Bradstreet	2.40 billion
Gannett Co.	1.96 billion
Tribune Co.	1.79 billion
Knight-Ridder Newspapers	1.66 billion
New York Times Co.	1.23 billion
Washington Post Co.	984 million
Dow Jones and Co.	966 million
Capital Cities	940 million

This information on a few of our media empires indicates their financial power or clout. And much of their income is from advertising revenue from companies seeking to sell their products or causes through commercials – sometimes euphemistically referred to by announcers as "messages from our sponsors."

In the pages that follow, I shall assess the power of the media – political, social, economic, and educational – with special heed given to the media's influence on children, youth, the family, and the larger society of which they are a part.

Media Frontiers, 1987-1995

An impressive example of media power and technical sophistication was provided in 1984 when communications networks provided millions of persons with "free tickets" to the Olympic Games at Sarajevo and Los Angeles. ABC Television designed its "wonder coverage" in Los Angeles, assembled and tested it in New York, then packed the equipment into 30 trailers and shipped them to Yugoslavia for the Winter Games. The impressive array of equipment included 70 TV monitors, 36 videotape machines, 150 miles of cable, and various satellite connections.[3]

At the Summer Games in Los Angeles later in the year, the media transmitted to our homes the excitement of the various events taking place in a 4,000-square-mile area in Southern California. Complicating coverage of the Games was the fact that the contestants from 51 nations spoke 83 languages, thus requiring interpreters to be on hand. Coverage of the events required 1,700 terminals with 14 computers to run or to monitor the terminals.

37

While coverage of the 1984 Olympics epitomized the sophistication of the media, other communication marvels are making their debut so frequently that it is virtually impossible to keep up with them. A few intriguing examples include:

- "Living wallpaper" made possible by huge TV screens thin enough to hang on the wall; and when no program is being watched, they display a variety of electronic "wallpaper graphics."
- The Lexicon 1200 Audio Time Compressor/Expander, which enables three out of 60 minutes to be salvaged for commercials or news breaks without losing any dialogue or action from a TV program.[4]
- The combination of computer and portable telephones plus "cellular radio," creating a mobile telephone network. This technology came into use during 1984-1985.[5]
- Elimination of costly installation and maintenance of phone lines in developing nations by means of satellite phone linkages.
- Deployment of the Intelsat VI satellites that simultaneously handle 33,000 phone conversations as well as carry programs on two TV channels between Europe and the United States.
- Recent developments in fiber optics that permit 240,000 simultaneous phone conversations to be carried between Washington and New York by means of a half-inch cable, which is twice as efficient as traditional copper wire and costs much less.[6]
- Satellite navigation for automobiles with dashboard print-outs of a map showing the driver's precise location.
- Electronic translation of an English manuscript into Arabic, Chinese, and other languages.
- Already established are the electronic newspaper, electronic banking, and electronic mail.
- A $180 million Infrared Astronomical Satellite (IRAS) or robot observatory with detectors so delicate that they can spot a small light bulb's glow on the planet Pluto — a distance of more than 3½ billion miles.

Something to be watched in the near future is one of the ventures in the $5 billion investment General Motors is making on its new Saturn automobile plant. This venture will link robots and computers that can "speak" to one another. If this two-way, machine-to-machine communication can be perfected: "exact specifications for an engine valve, once devised and tested on a computer can be transmitted to a computerized machine tool on the shop floor and manufactured. Flaws would be detected after just a few parts had been made, not after thousands had been installed."[7]

One final item that merits inclusion in our list of communications innovations is that in October 1985 the Grolier Publishing Company began marketing a compact disk (CD) encyclopedia. This single CD contains the
nine-million word, 21-volume contents of Grolier's well-known encyclopedia.[8] The CD can be used on personal computers.

Commercialism, Bias, and Politics

The media frontiers mentioned above are important for all educators to
understand, but it is in the elementary, secondary, and postsecondary curricula that the emerging role of the media is of consummate significance,
especially with respect to TV. The curriculum in many schools has yet to
be adapted to the micro milieu that is engulfing it. Teachers and their students need to be better informed about commercialism, gilded or slanted
news, and political influences in the media. Each of these aspects of the
media will be examined to show the ways in which the media are infusing
society and creating dilemmas for children, youth, and the family.[9]

Hype, hype, hype! The income figures for the media giants reported in
this chapter demonstrate the enormous financial stake they have in captur-
ing audiences. And their financial "take" is growing as a result of mergers
and expansion on the global scene. They engage in high-powered promotion, better known as "hype," the sheer intensity of which overwhelms the
viewer or reader.

The film industry is a prime example of bombarding promotion when
it comes to marketing its products. Major studios spend millions to publi-
cize their films; in the case of *The Return of the Jedi,* the sum exceeded
$10 million. The pay-off can be enormous when certain films gross sever-
al million in a week.

An interesting example of a spin-off promotion is illustrated in the popu-
lar film, *E.T., The Extra-Terrestrial.* The charming little visitor, E.T., is
lured from its hiding place by a young lad who used "Reese's Pieces" candy
as bait. The Hershey's Food Corporation's sales of the sweet zoomed 65%
in the month following the release of the film as youngsters hastened to
buy E.T.'s favorite food.

One example of promotion saturation was ABC Television's meticulous-
ly planned build-up of *The Day After,* a TV drama about the aftermath of
a nuclear war. That program had an estimated audience of 100 million people. Other examples are the debut of "Mr. T" at the January 1983 Super
Bowl and Coca-Cola's launching of its diet coke by renting the Radio City
Music Hall for 4,000 guests — at an estimated cost of $100,000. Some-
times, of course, media hoopla backfires, as when Coca-Cola introduced

its new Coke formula in 1985 with great fanfare only to have it rejected by the public.

American advertising has an enviable track record in selling products, but the excesses committed in the name of promotion tarnish our nation's image and often debase our language. Students need to learn in English and social studies classes what tricks the advertising wizards use to push products. They need to be able to distinguish slickness from sincerity, the truth from the fanciful.

Selected news. Because of the growing media infiltration unleashed by the microelectronic surround, it is important to help learners, young and old, understand the "selected news" and the artfully "enhanced truth" sometimes purveyed by the media to suit the purposes of commercial and political sponsors and those in seats of power. Pope John Paul II had this comment on the dangers of bias and innuendo: "Clearly placed emphasis, slanted interpretations, even loaded silences, are devices which can profoundly alter the significance of what is being communicated."

Even representatives of the media have begun to criticize sharply the practices of certain of their colleagues. At the time of the 1984 national political conventions in Dallas and San Francisco, Thomas Griffith commented on the arrogance and condescending coverage of the media, which assumed that "its own maunderings are more interesting than what is being said on the platform."[10] His most barbed remark was that CBS assumed that the audience would rather hear Dan Rather speak smugly in San Francisco than hear the hoarse Irish oratory of Tip O'Neill.

Donald D. Jones, one of the 70 ombudsmen for U.S. daily papers, averaged 40 complaints a day directed at the Kansas City *Star* and the Kansas City *Times*. Public mistrust, he said, resided in what was deemed to be: 1) inaccuracy, 2) arrogance, 3) unfairness, 4) disregard for privacy, 5) insensitivity with respect to race, religion, and sex, 6) overemphasis on criminal and bizarre happenings, and 7) bad writing. Jones also cited a 1983 Gallup poll reflecting greater hostility to the press than in any previous poll conducted by Gallup.[11]

S.M. Lipset of Stanford University says that by broadcasting bad news as it happens, TV "has helped maintain public negativism." Methodist Bishop James Armstrong, former president of the National Council of Churches, felt impelled to request time to rebut a segment on the news program, "60 Minutes," that contended that some NCC funds supported Marxist causes overseas. Perhaps the kindest remark I could find with regard to selected news was from Brown University professor David Marc, who noted that "Like the menu at McDonald's and the suits on the racks, the choices on the dial — and thus far the cable converter — are limited and guided."[12]

Overexposure by the media. The media also have been berated for providing too much coverage. A memorable example was the horde of 1,800 journalists who poured into the Irish village of Ballyporeen during President Reagan's visit to the home of his ancestors. The newscorps outnumbered the village's entire population by more than five to one!

Reaction to President Reagan's press ban during the initial stages of the 1983 Grenada invasion provides a good example of the public's resistance to "overkill" by the media. When NBC's John Chancellor criticized the President's press ban, it resulted in 500 phone calls to NBC supporting the ban by five to one. ABC's anchorman, Peter Jennings, said that 99% of his mail was from persons supporting President Reagan's decision to delay press coverage! As former *Washington Post* ombudsman Robert McCloskey saw it, "It may well be that the public reacted cumulatively with a judgment that the press had it coming."

In the Sean Connery movie, *Wrong Is Right,* he portrays a TV newscaster who makes entertainment out of disasters. His movie role was re-enacted in real life to some extent by the TV coverage of — some say meddling — the 17-day Beirut hijacking of a TWA 747 in 1985. Zbigniew Brzezinski, National Security Adviser in the Carter Administration, contends that the media, particularly TV, operate to the detriment of the country when hijacking or hostage taking are involved. He gives three reasons:

1. An essentially political confrontation, because of excessive media coverage, is transmitted into a personal drama that interferes with our government's ability to cope.
2. The bargaining capacity of the kidnappers is enhanced and the U.S. government is forced to seek some way of accommodating them.
3. The enemy is "humanized" by audiovisual contacts and victims are subject to manipulation.

Henry Kissinger went so far as to urge a news media blackout in Beirut rather than to give direct access to means of molding public opinion to the spokesmen for the hijackers.

Media access to breaking news is essential in a free society, but sometimes restraint — preferably self-imposed — is called for when covering crisis situations. The ethical dilemma posed when freedom of the press comes in conflict with national security is the kind of issue to which students should be exposed if they are to develop the insights needed to interpret and respond intelligently to the complexities of a global society.[13]

Politics and the media. Ward Just is one of many writers who have expressed concern recently about the role of the media in politics. Events often are arranged by television for television. He tells us, "the symbiotic relationship between the politicians and electronic mediators is so close as to resemble the chummiest of marriages: scratch one and the other bleeds."[14] Another view of the politics-media relationship is John M. Barry's quip: "The only thing people make in Washington is policy or gossip, and you usually don't know where one leaves off and the other begins."[15] This suggests that educators need to help students to identify bias, propaganda, and the loaded words that creep into interviews. Loaded words or selected photos and taped excerpts are intended to persuade an audience to accept a point of view that may or may not reflect the truth. As S.I. Hayakawa phrased it in *Language in Thought and Action,* there are "purr-words" and "snarl-words." As the media's influence grows, we need to recognize that the terms used by reporters (and politicians) can short-circuit our thinking.

How the media's "treatment" of the news is changing. Since the 1950s, there appears to have been a subtle shift by the media from a spirit of "cooperative patriotism" to one of skepticism. This is the conclusion of the M.I.T. News Study Group, which has charted news coverage on radio, TV, and the press. The M.I.T. group cites the media's withholding of information they possessed about the Cuban missile crisis in 1962 as an example of restraint. However, 20 years later, the M.I.T. group notes that ABC, NBC, and CBS news coverage has changed because of three key differences, which show "how far TV News has come in two decades — and how much Government has had to adjust to this changed media reality."[16]

1. The attitudes of journalists have changed with respect to cooperating with the government.

2. The press, including networks, have greater access to more information, thus allowing them to offer more complex interpretations of news events reflecting various points of view.

3. New communication technologies involving satellites and other electronic means provide almost instantaneous communication from any place in the world. (In 1962, CBS News got news from Cuba by hiring a plane to fly close enough to the island to get within range of Havana TV.)

An added caveat concerning the emerging role of the media was voiced recently by Reed Irvine, head of Accuracy in Media, Inc. While acknowledging the good job that some broadcast commentators are doing, Irvine believes that the real problem comes when journalists "start with a premise and then shape the evidence to fit that premise." "Documentaries," he added, "are very definitely designed to manipulate public opinion."[17] Clearly, educators and learners of every age need to be made aware of the implications of such developments in the media's treatment of the news.

42

Although my data generally support the good intentions and integrity of personnel in the media, some cautions are needed if the public is to be able to distinguish between facts and fiction. Guidance in interpreting what is presented is of supreme importance. As Richard Allen, former director of the National Security Council, said:

> Competition among the Washington press for air time and space is so great that sometimes an inadequate respect for the facts takes over. The willingness to publish leaks and views of "anonymous" sources leads to particular vicious situations that are grossly unfair to the object of the leak.[18]

David Halberstam, author of *The Best and the Brightest,* also has expressed concern about TV documentaries that obscure the truth. Using as an example the documentary, "Robert Kennedy and His Times," Halberstam expresses respect for the man but contempt for the media for its distortion and sanitization of Kennedy's role in the foreign policy of his brother's administration. For instance, Halberstam points out that no mention is made in the docudrama of the U.S.-sponsored invasion of the Bay of Pigs or of the U.S. role in the 1963 assassination of Ngo Dinh Diem, then president of South Vietnam.[19] I close this section on politics and the media with a candid statement from Henry Kissinger.

> Did I sometimes use the press? Yes. There is absolutely no doubt that when an official deals with the press, he is trying to "use" the press. And there is no doubt that when a reporter deals with an official, he is trying to "use" the official . . . the press must understand that the official is not there to please them but to achieve his objective.[20]

Stars of eventide: the TV anchors. This chapter on the growing power and influence of the media would be incomplete if comment were not made about the anchorpersons who, along with commercials, dominate our TV screens.

The first evening network news program made its appearance on CBS on 15 August 1948 with anchorman Douglas Edwards. By February 1949, NBC introduced John Cameron Swayze as anchorman for its evening news program, which nostalgic readers may remember as the "Camel News Caravan."[21] I, along with millions of Americans, was a dedicated fan of Walter Cronkite (the man most trusted by Americans). The current generation of "eventide stars" includes David Brinkley, Dan Rather, Roger Mudd, Peter Jennings, Barbara Walters, and Tom Brokaw.

In this era of increasingly sophisticated electronic media, educators must consider the implications of these proliferating evening news programs with their star-studded casts. Because of the stakes involved — billions of dollars from product sponsors – networks scramble to recruit and to keep on their rosters top-flight journalists who also project well as newsreaders. According to Matusow, "Networks are giving away salaries and editorial prerogatives that could not have been fantasized a decade ago."[22] My point is that with anchors' package deals sometimes pushing toward the $20 million dollar level, there is the potential for power grabs and an increase in the various forms of hype. Art Buchwald's April 1982 column, "My Latest Nightmare," puts it well when he says, "I'm frightened because the next big war is not going to be started by two countries but by an anchorman from one of the major TV networks."

Our students must be taught to interpret what they see and hear and to be aware of how greed, ambition, and power grabs sometimes can be invisible ingredients behind the TV cyclops' eye in our homes. While the news may sometimes be gilded, and while we may be increasingly exposed to injections of opinion in TV news, some respected persons in the media are making proposals that will help them do a better job. Tom Brokaw has made specific suggestions, a sampling of which follow:

1. Network news will never be an adequate replacement for a first-rate daily newspaper, a weekly news magazine or a periodical specializing in a specific subject. Instead, think of network news as a part of the information spectrum.

2. We need a wider stage. The time constraints on the evening news programs are suffocating. A one-hour network evening news program is an inspiration if television news is to fulfill its potential and its obligation to its audience.

3. Our most glaring shortcoming: We don't adequately examine the many sides of complicated subjects in a sufficiently broad context. An hour format should attract those who now avoid broadcast journalism with a 22-minute time limit after commercials are run.

4. Our coverage should focus on subjects that receive scant attention on many local news programs. We need to provide depth and breadth to the bits of information that bombard viewers all day.

5. It is television's role to do what print cannot do in conveying light and sound and unfiltered emotion including being bold enough to report stories where there are no pictures. New graphics technologies are making this possible.[23]

Concluding Comment

The micro milieu has made the varied forms of media so pervasive in our lives that it is difficult in this brief space to extricate and examine the media apart from society as whole. But of one thing I am convinced: Our curricula, broadly construed, should give more deliberate and more methodical attention to the topics so lightly touched above. There is work to be initiated and refined with every age group from early childhood through senior learners. Whether we move toward a better, more humane, global community or skid toward planetary catastrophe will, I believe, be determined by our skills, talent, and judgment in dealing with some of the issues, dilemmas, and opportunities discussed in this chapter.

Footnotes

1. Robert M. Hutchins, *The Conflict in Education* (New York: Harper, 1953), p. 102.
2. Reported in *U.S. News and World Report*, 1 April 1985, p. 48.
3. For more details, see Richard Stengel, "Your Ticket to the Games," *Time*, 13 February 1984, pp. 65-66. Also see George Plimpton, "Here's One Man's Meet," *Time*, 20 August 1984, pp. 76-79.
4. John Leo, "As Time Goes Bye-Bye," *Time*, 19 July 1982, p. 78.
5. "What Next? A World of Communications Wonders," *U.S. News and World Report*, April 1984, pp. 59-63.
6. Ibid., p. 61.
7. *U.S. News and World Report*, 5 August 1985, p. 24.
8. "Business Notes," *Time*, 29 July 1985, p. 64. Grolier also is developing an unabridged CD dictionary and a thesaurus. Also see Parker Rossman, "The Coming Great Electronic Encyclopedia," *The Futurist* 16 (August 1982): 53-57.
9. Fugitive materials (magazine and newspaper sources) were the primary source of the information summarized here. Not only were books on the topic rare, but they quickly become obsolete because of the speed with which media-related events occur.
10. *Time*, 20 August 1984, p. 105.
11. *Time*, 9 May 1983, p. 94.
12. David Marc, "Understanding Television," *Atlantic Monthly* (August 1984): 34.
13. For examples of apparent excesses of docudramas, see: 1) Julian Bond, "Television Toys with the Truth," circulated by the Newspaper Enterprise Association and published in various newspapers in February 1985; and 2) William A. Henry III, "The Dangers of Docudrama," *Time*, 25 February 1985, p. 95. Also recommended is Stewart Powell et al., "Do You Know What Your Children Are Listening To?" *U.S. News and World Report*, 28 October 1985, pp. 46-49.
14. Ward Just, "Politics: We Are the Hostages," *Atlantic Monthly* (April 1980): 100.
15. John M. Barry, "Washington's Powerhouse Press Corps," *Dun's Business Monthly* (July 1984): 26.
16. Edwin Diamond, "The Turning of TV News," *TV Guide*, 7 August 1982, pp. 4-8.
17. Cited in an interview published by *U.S. News and World Report*, 21 February 1983, p. 50.
18. Cited in *U.S. News and World Report*, 22 March 1982, p. 56.
19. David Halberstam, cited in *U.S. News and World Report*, 22 March 1982, p. 56.

20. Neil Hickey, "Henry Kissinger on Politics and TV Journalism," *TV Guide*, 2 April 1983, p. 3.

21. For a history of "anchored programs," see Barbara Matusow, *The Evening Stars* (New York: Houghton Mifflin, 1983).

22. Ibid.

23. Tom Brokaw, "Network News: How We Can Do It Better," *TV Guide*, 6 July 1985, pp. 4-7.

Part Two

Confronting New Realities in Education

One of the troubles of our age is that habits of thought cannot change as quickly as techniques, with the result that as skill increases, wisdom fades.
—Bertrand Russell

If the development of the human capacity for reflection is the essense of education . . . the mere accumulation of information is not education.
—Clarence Faust

Chapter 6
Issues, Dilemmas, and Opportunities in the Microelectronic Age

All the computers in the world won't help you if your unexamined and unconscious assumptions on the nature of reality are simply wrong in their basic conception. All the computers can do is to help you to be stupid in an expensive fashion.
— William Irwin Thompson[1]

The microelectronic age has brought us to a crossroads. If we have the right basic conceptions about the nature of reality, as Thompson urges, then we can make sound choices. Among our choices are: 1) an unprecedented opportunity for electronic global education, 2) increasing means of access to computerized knowledge, 3) greater freedom from toil as robots relieve us from many forms of physical labor, and 4) mental powers enhanced by artificial intelligence in the years immediately ahead. These four developments, many scholars speculate, can help us to overcome such ominous problems as resource depletion, overpopulation, and pollution, which threaten to degrade our quality of life.

I very much agree with Thompson that we must have sound conceptions of reality if we are to choose wisely in an era where our lives increasingly are influenced by the versatility of the silicon chip. At the beginning of the atomic era, it was Winston Churchill who commented: "The Stone Age may return on the gleaming wings of science!" With too many faulty conceptions, Churchill's observation might very well become reality!

In this chapter I shall deal with some of the issues and dilemmas of our time and the choices that they pose. As the terms are used here, an issue is a controversial problem or question to be resolved; a dilemma is a situation requiring a choice between unpleasant alternatives.

Issues: Making Wise Choices

Preserving creative, critical thinking. One of the persons from whom I sought advice when planning this book was the distinguished scholar, Elise Boulding, chairperson of the Sociology Department at Dartmouth College. She expressed concern lest educators fail to use computers wisely in the classroom. To illustrate her point she told me that Socrates was concerned lest the spread of the written word would undermine the oral tradition. In the *Phaedrus* Socrates also said that writing threatened to destroy memory. "Will the computer tend to destroy thinking as well?" asks Boulding.[2] I think that she has identified a key issue; namely, how best to use computers to sustain and expand the power of creative thinking rather than to limit it.

Joseph Weizenbaum, a specialist in the field of artificial intelligence at M.I.T. and inventor of the famous Eliza computer program, is another respected scholar who warns that computers can undermine thinking. In an interview in *Le Nouvel Observateur,* Weizenbaum was asked if he thought France was making a mistake by trying to put computers in everyone's hands. (The interviewer's question was in reference to the French post office's recent campaign to supply home terminals to replace telephone directories and provide access to information services. By autumn 1984 the service had more than 500,000 subscribers.)

> If that is what France is doing, then, yes, it's making a mistake. The temptation to send in computers wherever there is a problem is great. There's hunger in the Third World. So computerize. The schools are in trouble. So bring in computers. The introduction of the computer into any problem area, be it medicine, education, or whatever, usually creates the impression that grievous deficiencies are being corrected, that something is being done. But often its principal effect is to push problems even further into obscurity – to avoid confrontation with the need for fundamentally critical thinking.[3]

A technological "fix" will solve few, if any, of our contemporary global problems unless used to support the exercise of our multiple intelligences. Nor will a New Age be brought about by merely proclaiming the virtues of computers. Rather, it will require that our powers of critical thinking be focal points of renewed interest and vigor in the classroom and in society.

Using microcomputers simply to retrieve information or to reinforce skills heretofore presented on chalkboards, in books, or by a teacher's lectures is not enough. Learners also must be helped to develop their creative imaginations. *Time* (16 September 1985) reported that there were more than one million computers in U.S. classrooms, up from 630,000 the previous year. Will they be used in ways that will help students to deal with social and environmental problems that demand creative solutions?

The frozen curriculum. The microcomputer holds enormous potential for lubricating learning, but it also can lead to instructional malpractice by "freezing" program development in out-of-date or inadequate software. This occurs through such inappropriate use of software as the following:

1. Limiting computer use to workbook-type drill in basic skills in reading and mathematics.

2. Indiscriminate use of software without considering wide-ranging individual differences at every age level.

3. Failure to encourage continuing development of software by the faculty.

4. Overinvesting in both hardware and software and requiring them to be used for five or more years in order to amortize costs.

5. Limiting teacher initiative by requiring tests based on inadequate software programs, which fail to stimulate creative and critical thinking.

6. Overuse of computers, which could impoverish the imagination of some learners, especially children who are started on computer learning tasks at an early age.[4]

Another computer-related issue is posed by the impending teacher shortage, which was dramatized in late summer of 1985 when Los Angeles and New York City had to recruit approximately 5,000 teachers that fall. The National Education Association estimates as many as a million new teachers will be needed during the 1990s as the children of baby-boom era parents enter the schools. With this many new teachers needed, there is concern that many will be hired without adequate training and that computer-frozen materials will be used as a means of providing cheap and quick instruction.

A final issue in our sampling is how to deal with the allocation of computers to the students who most need them but have least access to them.

A Sampling of Dilemmas: Making Some Hard Choices

Dilemmas created by our microelectronic surround require policy decisions that are likely to be difficult and sometimes controversial. The sample discussed here includes: problems of computer-related fraud or thievery, the antics of pranksters and youthful hackers, threats to individual privacy, electronic pollution of communication systems, information overload or "infoglut," and problems with two-way or interactive TV.

Added to the above list are those dilemmas imposed on the family by the microelectronic surround, such as children's exposure on TV to explicit sex and violence, the blurring of child and adult roles, and the inequity

51

among families in their ability to purchase computer equipment. Families already are having to cope with financial obligations imposed by a growing number of universities that require students to own personal computers.

The final dilemma discussed here is the enormous problems that could be created by the explosion of even a single nuclear warhead, resulting in an electromagnetic pluse (EMP) capable of knocking out both global computer memory banks and many digital circuits in electronic equipment.

Electronic fraud and vandalism. Among my files containing hundreds of clippings from newspapers and journals, none bulge more than those that deal with various forms of thievery, fraud, and dangerous pranks of mischievous computer buffs, many of whom are in their teens or early twenties. A small sample of headlines from my files tells a story of endemic fraud and vandalism.

> Thieves steal credit file computer code. Credit and personal data on 90 million Americans were obtained when computer hackers stole a code number from TRW Information Services in suburban Los Angeles. *Indianapolis Star* (22 June 1984, p. 1).

> Stirling University discovers that details of all its computerized administrative records had been"cracked." *The Scotsman* (23 December 1982, p. 5).

> Of 275 businesses and agencies polled by the American Bar Association, 27% concluded that they had lost an estimated half-billion dollars in one year due to computer crime in 1984. Nationwide, the losses are staggering. One unscrupulous bank computer operator with the proper code word wired $10.2 million from another bank to his Swiss account. *U.S. News and World Report* (25 June 1985, p. 8).

Another disturbing development has been the theft and vandalism perpetrated by youth such as the Milwaukee "414 Gang" and a group of seven New Jersey teenagers. *Time* (29 July 1985) reported that the New Jersey youths were arrested for using home computers and telephone hookups to commit theft. They had acquired at least $30,000 in computer equipment and disks, exchanged stolen credit card numbers, bypassed long distance phone fees (known as "phreaking" in hacker jargon), and even managed to shift the orbit of one or more communications satellites.

The Milwaukee group included some Explorer Scouts from a troop sponsored by a well-meaning IBM employee. *Newsweek* (5 September 1983) reported that an initial investigation by the FBI indicated that the "414

Gang" were suspected of having entered more than 60 business and government computer systems in the United States and Canada, including one at the Los Alamos National Laboratory! What alarms many security experts is that the break-ins were not dazzling technological feats. For instance, all it took to penetrate the computers at Sloan-Kettering Cancer Center, where 250 patients were monitored by a medical computer service, was a home computer, a modem, a push-button phone, and a modest degree of computer literacy. Los Alamos proved to be so computer vulnerable that Defense Secretary Casper Weinberger subsequently was obliged to order a high-level study of security at all U.S. intelligence and military centers by senior Pentagon and CIA officials.

A Little Rock, Arkansas, high school hacker broke into his school's computerized records in 1984 and changed his grades and those of some friends. A 13-year-old in Columbia, Maryland, used stolen credit card numbers and telephoned orders for $3,000 to $4,000 worth of goods, which were delivered to unoccupied homes in the vicinity of his neighborhood. Whether you label such acts as criminal (which they are) or merely pranks by mischievous and clever teenagers, they raise serious issues about the right to privacy in our microelectronic era.

A development of particular concern to parents are the home electronic "bulletin boards" run by some hackers, most of whom are teenage boys from affluent homes.[5] The bulletin boards are computer networks on which information can be swapped. More than 1,000 electronic bulletin board networks were operating by 1985 providing useful and important information to those in the business and academic world. But this technological marvel can be abused by hackers when they use it to transmit messages on such topics as techniques for picking locks, how to use someone else's credit card, sexually explicit material from pornographic magazines, or how to make free long-distance calls.

Invasion of privacy. The dilemma created by the computer is that it can be a useful servant or a nosy pest.[6] In 1984 it was estimated that on the average, a U.S. citizen's name was listed on 70 private, federal, state, and local files. According to Joseph L. Galloway, on a typical day every name passes from one computer to another five times.[7] Then there is the sheer annoyance of being bombarded with third-class mail generated from computer address lists that can be purchased from many sources.

Increasingly, computer files are being used by agencies for investigating kidnappings, murders, terrorism, and espionage. John Shattuck, a former American Civil Liberties Union official, stated our privacy dilemma succinctly when he said, "Technology is now outstripping the law."[8]

The table below shows the extent of personal data available in files of various agenices in the United States. While the Freedom of Information and Privacy Act of 1974 entitles citizens to see their government files (except for a few security matters) and to challenge data they consider inaccurate, there is reason for concern if these files are used for exploitation by the unscrupulous.

A Sampling of Agencies in the U.S. with Personal Data Files[9]

Agency	Number of Individual Files (1984)
Selective Service	11 million men
Medical Information Bureau	12 million patients
Private Investigative Agencies	14 million annual reports
Criminal Records	60 million files
Credit Bureaus	150 million subjects
State Motor Vehicle Agencies	152 million licensed drivers
U.S. Government Agencies	3.8 billion names
Total Files	4.8 billion

Electronic pollution. Electronic pollution is a nuisance by-product of our technology. Often called "noise" or "hash" by technicians, electronic pollution is becoming more and more common as the use of computer technology multiplies. The problem is caused by radiation from electronic equipment.

For example, video game centers have drowned out highway patrol transmissions; and stray radiations from TV cameras interrupted communications between the astronauts on our first space shuttle and their ground controllers. Even encephalograms are becoming more difficult to take because of the increase in radiation from micro-equipment used in hospitals for more and more purposes.

We have long put up with radio static and interference on TV screens. But the tiny computer chips used in today's electronic devices can be disturbed by external radiation with consequences far more serious than the static problems of radio. Thus, one of our many dilemmas is deciding what should be permissible standards with respect to radiation from electronic devices.

Information overload. Overexposure by the media or "infoglut"[10] was discussed in Chapter 5. The dilemma is how to ensure open access to information in a democracy without being swamped by more than it is possible to absorb. Anthony Smith, a British expert on information technology and the author of *Goodbye Gutenberg,* has noted that students' greater access to information must be accompanied by training in selective viewing beginning at a very young age.[11]

Interactive TV. Qube, an interactive or two-way TV system, was introduced in the late 1970s in Columbus, Ohio. It is a cable system that enables viewers to "talk back" to the tube. Using a keypad the size of a small hand calculator, a viewer communicates directly with a computer that continually monitors the set. Every few seconds it records the sets linked to it, and thus can determine to which specific channel each set is tuned. In a sense, this is a form of invasion of privacy. In a few years the Columbus Qube system will have more than 50,000 sets hooked to it. The system has spread in recent years to such cities as Cincinnati, Dallas, St. Louis, Houston, New Orleans, Omaha, and San Diego.

Interactive TV systems can bring an abundance of services to the home (games, encyclopedic information, entertainment, video catalogs), but it has yet to be established whether the new interactive "telecommunity" that Alvin Toffler described in *The Third Wave* will result in greater family bonding or will lead to greater personal isolation within the home. Joshua Meyrowitz contends that the electronic media are having an impact on family roles:

> Because of TV, children today know much more about adult behavior, men and women are exposed to each other's strategies and domains. . . . The result has been a shattering of roles . . . and barriers that once kept things in their place.[12]

Also, Jean Bethke Elshtain warns us about the manipulative power of interactive TV:

> Advocates of interactive TV systems . . . view these technologies as making our society more democratic. But they do not understand the nature of real democracy, which they confuse with the plebecite system. Plebecitism is compatible with authoritarian politics because opinion can be easily manipulated. A truly democratic policy involves a deliberative process. The ersatz participation of interactive TV is at odds with this democratic ideal.[13]

The showing of pornography on interactive TV and other cable systems creates another kind of dilemma for families. Also, the recent sales boom in videocassettes and VCRs[14] creates a problem for families with children who can watch X-rated videos in the home environment.[15] However, one can't help but wonder what "community standards" for obscenity are when one reads the incident below.

When an adult theater owner was taken to court on obscenity charges for showing *Taxi Girls,* he asked his attorney to subpoena Qube's list of subscribers who had tuned in on the same film. Viewers' names were not turned over to the court, but the number of viewers was provided. It turns out that far more citizens saw *Taxi Girls* on the Qube cable (more than half of the subscribers' sets were tuned in) than saw the film at the adult movie theater!

Sex and violence on the TV screen. Children need to experience warmth, love, and tenderness if they are to achieve a normal wholesome development. The dilemma for parents is how to counteract the inundation of sex and violence their children see on TV. Sexual innuendoes, vulgarity, and bedroom scenes on TV do not make much sense to younger children and give distorted ideas about sex to older learners. Until networks exercise better taste in program content, parents will need to exercise more control in determining what their children view.

The disappearance of childhood. Neil Postman argues convincingly that TV is having a "disastrous influence" on children, shortening the attention span and "eroding to a considerable extent, their linguistic powers and their ability to handle mathematical symbolism." He goes on to point out that TV robs children of their childhood by communicating the same information to everyone, thus eliminating a number of important distinctions between children and adults. Postman tells us that as childhood vanishes prematurely, there is an adverse effect on the family.[16]

The have and have-not chasm. Another dilemma facing parents is their ability to purchase microcomputers and other microelectronic gear. This concern is reflected in the titles of recent articles, such as "Will the rich get smarter while the poor play video games?"[17] and "Sophisticated computer use said tied to wealth."[18] The data suggest that affluent families and the schools their children attend are getting a more nutritious diet of micro technologies than the poor families and the schools their children attend.

According to a U.S. Education Department report, disadvantaged and minority students are likely to be handicapped with respect to computer availability. About twice as much computer time per week was available in schools with small minority enrollments as in schools with large minority enrollments.[19] Even when computers are available, 80% of the teachers are likely to use them for drill and practice rather than higher order thinking.

The EMP menace. In July 1962 the United States launched its last above-ground nuclear bomb. The warhead turned into a ball of nuclear fire after it was lofted 248 miles above Johnston Atoll, located 800 miles southwest of Hawaii. Instantaneously in Honolulu and in other areas in the Hawaiian Islands, power lines went dead, street lights went out, fuses were blown. We later learned that this electronic chaos was the result of an intense electromagnetic pulse (EMP).[20]

A panel assembled by the National Research Council reported that EMP power from a nuclear explosion is so great it could "render unprotected

56

electronic equipment and systems inoperative over an area as large as the continental United States."[21] Brigadier General Sidney Davis in 1985 stated: "While EMP has no known effect on personnel, it can be the most devastating of all nuclear effects . . . because of the enormously large area affected by a single nuclear burst."[22]

EMP has been likened to a very strong radio signal of short duration somewhat similar to lightning; and it is much more powerful than lightning. A single nuclear explosion 300 miles above a central state such as Nebraska would send out an EMP energy surge that could render impotent much of America's electronic gear for thousands of miles in all directions. Fortunately, EMP does not harm humans; they cannot hear, feel, or see the pulse. However, many persons might be killed or injured by the failure of electronic equipment on which we have become so dependent.[23]

Educators as well as the general public must become aware of the potential threat that EMP poses and should lend their support to worldwide disarmament efforts so that the threat is never realized.

The Opportunity Threshold

The issues and dilemmas imposed by the microelectronic age that have been discussed in this chapter could lead one to a sense of despair. But balancing this despair is the threshold of opportunity provided by the technological marvels of the microelectronic age — opportunities to make the human mind a new frontier to be explored and opened. It is the human mind, wisely used, that can make the microelectronic support system we are creating a positive force in our future.

I close with some summary thoughts about how educators might contribute to the resolution of the issues and dilemmas discussed in this chapter.

- Encourage TV networks to offer programs that do not dwell on society's blemishes.
- Work to remove class barriers in our society where there is constant jockeying for privilege.
- Do not use microcomputers as tools for rote learning; otherwise there may never be another Homer, Socrates, or Shakespeare produced.
- Cherish diversified thinking; whenever everyone thinks alike, no one thinks very much.
- Respect the threads that bind the seams of history for they hold together the insights of scholars as well as the fantasies of knaves.
- Be patient if our quest for knowledge sometimes seems slow, even with the help of computers. Remember, we only can see the clock's second hand move.

- Avoid using computers to fill all young minds with the same facts. A world of intellectually cloned pupils will not be very interesting.
- When attacking the problems imposed by the microelectronic age, endeavor to identify the factors that created them in the first place.
- Help young learners to recognize that computers, like hand calculators, sometimes help us to make intellectual errors more quickly.
- Do not let the authority of the mind be leached away by the microchip. Each has a different function.
- When building or remodeling a school, don't let yourself develop an "edifice complex" with respect to electronic gear.
- When youngsters are using a computer, remind them that the search for truth is as precious as possessing it.
- Our electronic devices may serve as the "connective tissue" for our minds, but they do not replace the brains, which are the "germ plasm" of our society.

Footnotes

1. William Irwin Thompson, *At the Edge of History* (New York: Harper Colophon, 1972), p. 165.
2. Elise Boulding, personal correspondence. Also see, Elise Boulding, "The Social Imagination and the Crisis of Human Futures: A North American Perspective," paper presented at the U.N. University Symposium on "Crisis, Culture and Innovation in the Western World," Milan, Italy, 2-5 November 1982.
3. Cited in *Harper's Magazine*, 22 March 1984.
4. For a summary of various additional problems, see Fred M. Hechinger, "Harsh Charges Against Computers," *New York Times*, 10 July 1984, page C-10.
5. For a more detailed account, see "The Shadowy Word of Computer Hackers," *U.S. News and World Report*, 3 June 1985, pp. 58-60.
6. For succinct statements of the problem, see Gary T. Marx, "The Surveillance Society," *The Futurist* 19 (June 1985): 21-26; and Joseph L. Galloway, "How Your Privacy Is Being Stripped Away," *U.S. News and World Report*, 30 April 1984, pp. 46-48.
7. Galloway, op. cit., p. 46.
8. Cited in *Time*, 14 January 1985, p. 58.
9. Galloway, op. cit.
10. A term coined by Michael Marien, editor of *Future Survey*.
11. Cited in *U.S. News and World Report*, 24 November 1980, p. 78.
12. Joshua Meyrowitz, *No Sense of Place: The Impact of Electronic Media on Social Behavior* (New York: Oxford University Press, 1985).
13. Jean Bethke Elshtain, "Interactive TV: Democracy and the QUBE Tube," *The Nation*, 7 August 1982, p. 108.
14. Sales data for 1984 indicated that more than 7 million VCRs and 113.5 million videocassettes were shipped to retailers.

15. Some VCR dealers now carry equipment that parents can use to prevent children from tuning to X-rated channels.

16. Neil Postman, "The Day Our Children Disappear: Predictions of a Media Ecologist." *Phi Delta Kappan* (January 1981): pp. 382-86.

17. *Time,* 15 November 1982, p. 69.

18. *Education Week,* 16 November 1983, p. 10.

19. Ibid.

20. Information regarding the EMP is taken from various sources: the U.S. Army Nuclear and Chemical Agency, the National Research Council associated with the National Academy of Sciences, and material published by the American Association for the Advancement of Science.

21. National Academy of Sciences report cited by the New York Times News Service, "Scientists seek ways to protect us from electromagnetic pulse." Quoted in the *Chicago Sunday Tribune,* 26 August 1984, Section 6, page 9.

22. Sidney Davis, "EMP Mitigation for Field Equipment," *Bulletin of the U.S. Army Nuclear and Chemical Agency* (Springfield, Va.: Department of the Army, May 1985), p. 3.

23. For one of the most succinct statements on the nature and implications of EMP, see William J. Broad, "The Chaos Factor," *Science* (January/February 1983): 41-49. For a fictional account of EMP effects generated by nuclear explosions, see Whitley Streiber and James Kunetka, *Warday* (New York: Holt, Rinehart and Winston, 1984). It describes the experiences of two reporters in the days and months after America's communications systems are blacked out by EMP.

Chapter 7
Redesigning Education for a
High-Tech Society

*If we care to look we can foresee growing knowledge, growing order,
and presently a deliberate improvement . . . of the [human] race.*

*It is possible to believe that all the past is but the beginning of a
beginning, and that all that is and has been is but the twilight of the
dawn.*

—H.G. Wells[1]

The improvement of educational opportunity in America has a long and
fascinating history, beginning in 1642 with enactment of the Massachusetts
General Education Law and continuing up to the present. With each cycle
of education reform came recommendations by those highly critical of
schooling in the United States. In the 1950s it was Arthur Bestor, Hyman
Rickover, and Rudolf Flesch. In the 1960s came proposals for curriculum
reforms in the post-Sputnik era as well as the rhetoric of the so-called
"Romantic" critics by such writers as John Holt, Jonathan Kozol, and James
Herndon. The 1980s have witnessed a blizzard of reform reports, most nota-
bly *A Nation at Risk* (1983) by the National Commission on Excellence
in Education, but also from other groups or committees. All of these reports
contain harsh — and sometimes scathing — critiques of the quality of our
schools. The appendix contains summaries of 18 recent reports on education reform.

Education Reforms in Historical Perspective

Since the 17th century, reform efforts to improve our schools have reflected a faith in the power of education. As New York Governor DeWitt
Clinton phrased it in 1826, "The first duty of government and the surest

evidence of good government is the encouragement of education." Beginning in Massachusetts in 1642, reforms reflected the idea that universal education was essential to the well-being of the state. A central idea in early proposals was that the state could tax citizens to support schools. Also, the state could enforce school attendance laws. With mandatory secondary education came support for education beyond the level of basic skills.

Three NEA committees occupy a prominent place in the history of education reform: the Committee of Ten (1892), the Committee of Fifteen (1893), and the Committee of Twelve (1895). The Committee of Ten, chaired by Harvard president Charles W. Elliot, maintained that it did not matter what subjects a student studied as long as they provided strong mental training. It proposed a unit system of instruction based on a given number of recitations in a fixed weekly schedule. Another recommendation was a six-year elementary program to replace the existing eight-year program so that secondary-level courses in mathematics, science, and foreign languages could be begun sooner. Some recommendations of the Committee of Ten anticipated reforms proposed during the 1980s. Among them were improved teacher preparation, curriculum revision, and better articulation of school programs from kindergarten through postsecondary education.

The Committee of Fifteen Report proposed such reforms as a more balanced curriculum and better correlation of subject matter. It also recommended that a child's environment should be a factor in the selection of subject matter. The limited preparation of teachers a century ago was reflected in the recommendation that elementary teachers should have completed high school and secondary school teachers should have completed college. These reports of the Committee of Ten and Committee of Fifteen were influential in the creation of the College Entrance Examination Board in 1900; and subsequently secondary schools began to modify their curricula to meet the requirements for admission to college.

The Committee of Twelve recommended that secondary education begin with grade seven, thus laying the basis for what was to become the three-year junior high school. It also recommended that the school day be lengthened to allow time for supervised study – an idea reiterated more than 80 years later in *A Nation at Risk* with its proposal for seven-hour school days.

The founding of the Progressive Education Association in 1919 and the so-called "scientific" or testing movement, which peaked in the 1920s, were other powerful forces influencing education reform.[2]

The roster of reform groups and efforts touched on in the preceding paragraphs are illustrative rather than comprehensive. They are included to make the point that, for the most part, they tended to emphasize repairs needed in faulty educational policies and practices; or they were designed to improve existing practices in curriculum and instruction. A scrutiny of the reform proposals of the 1980s reveals that, for the most part, their recommendations also call for strengthening education by improving things as they are.

While acknowledging the positive contributions of reform groups past and present, I am concerned because recent reform proposals tend to dwell on "patching up" the existing system rather than *redesigning* the structure of our schools for the emerging microelectronic era. John Dewey spoke to the issue of reform versus redesign 50 years ago in the context of providing mass education.

> As I see the matter, there are three alternative ways of meeting the problem. We may continue the course we have taken in the past . . . one of improvisation and drift. We may deliberately adopt the policy of selective restriction. Or we may attempt a deliberate rethinking of our entire educational philosophy and reorganize our educational practice to meet the conditions imposed by what has become, in fact, mass education.[3]

Dewey's advice about "rethinking" our educational philosophy and "reorganizing" our educational practice could not be more pertinent today as we enter the microelectronic age.

Some Recent Efforts in Redesigning Education

Of the many reform reports released in the 1980s, one of the few that suggests new designs in education has been virtually ignored since its publication a few months before *A Nation at Risk* was released in 1983. This challenging document, titled *Informational Technology and Its Impact on American Education,* was prepared by the Office of Technology Assessment (OTA) for a subcommittee of the House Committee on Science and Technology.[4]

The OTA report suggests that a *redesign* of American education is in order rather than such pedestrian *reforms* as a longer school year or 60 minutes of math and 30 minutes of science instruction per day. Its two major conclusions are:

> 1. The so-called information revolution . . . is profoundly affecting American education. It is changing what needs to be learned, who needs to learn it, who will provide it, and how it will be provided and paid for. . . .
> 2. Information technology can potentially improve and enrich the educational services that traditional educational institutions provide,

distribute education and training into new environments such as the home and office, and reach new clients such as handicapped or homebound persons, and teach job-related skills in the use of technology.[5]

A second major report calling for redesigning or restructuring American education, particularly teacher education, is *A Nation Prepared: Teachers for the 21st Century*. Prepared by the Carnegie Task Force on Teaching as a Profession and released in May 1986, this report, in contrast to the OTA report, received lavish media attention. Among its major recommendations making the headlines are:

1. Requiring a bachelor's degree in arts and sciences as a prerequisite for the professional study of teaching in a graduate program in education leading to the master's degree.

2. Introducing the "lead teacher" concept as a way of restructuring the teaching force, using teachers of proven ability in the redesign of schools.

3. Establishing competitive salaries reaching $40,000 or more with a $65,000 to $80,000 range for lead teachers.

4. Creating a National Board for Professional Teaching Standards.

Albert Shanker, president of the American Federation of Teachers and a member of the Carnegie Task Force, has the following to say about the issue of reform versus redesign:

> The recent reform effort, which has been good, has merely been aimed at correcting the abuses of the 1960s. Carnegie says: How can we go beyond the 1950s to build schools that we will need for the next century? We must do more than put a new coat of paint on an old structure.[6]

A third significant report dealing with the redesign of education is *Transforming American Education: Reducing the Risk to the Nation*. Released in the spring of 1986, this report was prepared by a task force appointed in 1984 by former Secretary of Education Terrel Bell. The report looks at the changing role of the school resulting from the impact of "electronic, information age technology" and calls for redesigning or transforming education in ways that take into account the impact of microelectronic technology.

If we are to do more than "put a new coat of paint on an old structure," as Shanker insists we must do, then it seems appropriate to explore possible structures for the redesign of education for the emerging microelectronic age.

Redesign of Education: Some Speculations

The term "redesign," as used here, refers to basic changes in the structure and policies that govern educational practices in the United States. I have selected three broad topics as exemplars from among many that might be considered in redesigning schools for the world of tomorrow. They are: 1) coping with mass education and the wide range of ability among learners; 2) cooperation with the business world, including retraining persons who lose their jobs because of technological innovations; and 3) the school environment as a teaching aid. Comments on possible developments in school architecture will be discussed in Chapter VIII.

Coping with mass education. After World War I, with the passage of compulsory attendance laws, secondary education was becoming universal in America. One result was that secondary schools were no longer elitist institutions. Another was that secondary schools had to serve students with a much wider range of intellectual ability.

To deal with the range in ability in children of the same age, it is proposed that we begin by redesigning early childhood education. Children could be enrolled — regardless of their chronological age — whenever they reach a developmental level of the average four-year-old in what would essentially be a two-year kindergarten program. They would remain in this pre-primary school group from one to three years until they had acquired the developmental characteristics of the average six-year-old. In effect, this would increase the age spread in grade one but decrease the range in ability. The same developmental approach would apply in the primary grades. Young learners would remain in grades 1 to 4 until they could perform the skills expected of 10- or 11-year-olds when entering grade five. There would be no annual mass promotions; rather, there would be periodic transitions to a more advanced group in the learning continuum as children acquired higher levels of academic skills.[7]

Cooperation with the business community. In view of the $60 billion dollars spent in 1985 by the business world for education and training, redesigning education must take into account the inroads business and industry has made into the virtual educational monopoly our schools had attained in the 1950s. At secondary and postsecondary levels substantial redesign will be required in order to produce graduates equipped to survive in changing times. Opportunities here include: 1) retraining adults who are displaced by technology, 2) preparing teachers to work with adult learners who have been displaced by new technology or to work in nursery education in daycare centers at offices and factories where a growing number of working mothers are employed; 3) providing training in special technical skills needed in the silicon age; and 4) working with the business community to provide remedial work in basic math and communication skills, which seem to elude a number of secondary school graduates.

The school environment as a teaching aid. An important but neglected element in most reform proposals is their failure to consider redesigning the school environment so that the environment itself becomes an important teaching aid. Two aspects of school environment that need greater emphasis in redesigning education are *experience/exposure learning* and *service learning.*

Experience/exposure learning calls for curricular redesign that permits adolescents to encounter a wider variety of experiences than are usually found in the standard secondary school curriculum. Below are some kinds of experience/exposure learning I have in mind that can occur within the school environment.

1. An introduction to basic uses of the computer, including familiarity with hardware, software, and computer languages.
2. The use of networking for information retrieval.
3. Personal typing and word-processor instruction.
4. Substance-abuse education.
5. Experience with younger children by helping on school playgrounds or serving as junior paraprofessionals in a nursery school.
6. Art and shop experiences culminating in creative production.
7. Consumer education, including detecting bias in news and propaganda in commercials.
8. Tutoring younger children.
9. Participation in dramatics or forensic activity for presentation to parents or classmates.

For these kinds of experience/exposure to occur, educators will need to create new designs in organizational structure, new designs that go beyond reforms that merely enhance current practice. Creating the new designs can be facilitated by careful architectural planning when remodeling a school plant or building a new one. In short, the curriculum and teaching practices should determine the nature of the school environment.

Service learning involves student participation in the real world of work, with their activities (some with financial compensation) sponsored or brokered by the school and coordinated with parents. Service learning would be primarily for older adolescents but could also include those in post-secondary institutions, which would extend the age range upward to mature learners past 30. Scheduling arrangements would need to be more flexible and might involve a semester or even an academic year off to work in business, industry, social agencies, and institutions.[8]

Minimum wage legislation, compulsory attendance laws, and academic credit requirements would need to be modified to permit service learning in the world of work. This could be arranged initially in a few pilot schools as an experiment. As service learning proved its worth, it seems likely that legislators at state and federal levels would modify or introduce laws to encourage greater academic flexibility.

Following is a sampling of service learning activities that might be brokered by a secondary school or postsecondary institution:

1. Working in retirement homes or agencies for the handicapped; serving as junior paraprofessionals in school or industry nursery school programs.

2. Tutoring peers in the use of microcomputers, in retrieving network information.

3. Assisting in the library in the use of computerized reference materials, shelving books, telling or reading stories to young children.

4. Helping in federal, state, or local agencies in such areas as food stamp distribution and animal shelter maintenance.

5. Working in post offices and public parks during peak seasons.

6. Assisting in hospitals, reading to patients, or playing games in pediatric wards.

7. Participating in political campaign activities for the party of choice.

8. Working on community welfare programs such as food distribution to the needy.

9. Assisting youth-serving organizations such as scouting, YWCA, and YMCA and serving as staff members in summer camps run by such groups.

10. Working with agencies and organizations engaged in antipollution and cleanup projects.

11. Working for compensation but under school supervision in varied settings such as filling stations or offices.

The illustrations of experience/exposure and service learning suggested above should pave the way for more flexible postsecondary programs such as the tech-prep concept. There is no reason why persons cannot be admitted to non-degree programs as special students or "mature learners" without having to meet conventional college entrance requirements. Such a policy would provide a flexible learning continuum of lifelong learning. With flexible admission requirements, higher education could serve learners of all ages, including persons with personal computers enrolled in electronic university courses. These persons "attend" class at a time of their choice via microelectronic channels, which are increasing in number and variety.

All the ideas for flexible organization presented here are possible using what are largely existing educational resources but will require more versatile, creative designs to widen and to enrich personal experience. The designs would neither replace current faculties nor demand extensive expanding or rebuilding of school plants. Expanding experience/exposures, contributing one's service, and engaging in part-time employment simply offer new approaches within the context of U.S. educational resources.

Concluding Comment

The microelectronic age has created, and will continue to create, substantive changes in the realms of production, marketing, home life, work, leisure, access to information, politics, global communications, and international relations. The emerging age promises to be an intriguing mix of problems and opportunities, a blend of satisfactions and frustrations. While future developments cannot be predicted with precision, it already has become evident that many changes are mandated for education.

It has been my thesis in this chapter that we must do more than refine existing policies and practices of schooling. We will need new organizational and curriculum structures, greater variety of educational offerings, and more personalized programs to prepare persons for life in a world bereft of old certainties. Experience/exposure and service learning as well as greater flexibility in postsecondary and corporate education are proposed not as *the* answer to future needs but as examples of possible futures in education that imaginative teachers can devise.

Chapter 8 explores some of the changes in the curriculum that the micromillennium will mandate for schools of tomorrow.

Footnotes

1. H.G. Wells, "The Discovery of the Future." First published in *The Smithsonian Report* (1902). Reprinted, with an introduction by Edward Cornish, in *Futures Research Quarterly* (Summer 1985): 54-73.

2. Readers interested in a scholarly account of early American reform movements should read Lowry W. Harding's summary in Chapters VIII and IX in *The Thirteenth Yearbook of the John Dewey Society* (New York: Harper, 1953).

3. John Dewey, "The Integrity of Education," *Education Digest* 2 (November 1935): 1-3.

4. Copies of the OTA report may be obtained from the Superintendent of Documents, U.S. Government Printing Office, Washington, D.C. 20402. GPO stock number 052-003-00888-2.

5. From the foreword to the OTA report by John H. Gibbons, p. 3.

6. *U.S. News and World Report* interview, 26 May 1986, p. 57.

7. For a discussion of the continuum concept, see H.G. Shane, *The Educational Significance of the Future* (Bloomington, Ind.: Phi Delta Kappa Educational Foundation, 1973). Also recommended: Mark D. Danner et al., "How Not to Fix the Schools: Grading the Educational Reformers," *Harper's* (February 1986): 39-51.

8. For a classic study of the schools' efforts, as far back as the 1930s, to find worthy school-community work activities, see Paul R. Hanna, *Youth Serves the Community* (New York: D. Appleton-Century, 1936).

Chapter 8
Curriculum Change for the
Microelectronic Age

The good school is that form of community life in which all those agencies are concentrated that will be most effective in bringing the child to share in the inherited resources of the race.
　　　　　　　　　　　　　　　—John Dewey
　　　　　　　　　　　　　　　My Pedagogic Creed (1897)

The microelectronic age has the potential for helping all of us to share in the inherited and accumulating resources of humankind. However, the computer and its peripherals will not automatically thrust improved human resources into our minds or hands. As pointed out in the Association for Supervision and Curriculum Development newsletter, *Update,*[1] a number of problems need to be solved if the computer is to become the ally and educational partner envisioned by its enthusiasts. Among the problems are: 1) lack of access to computers by those who could benefit most, 2) uncertainty as to how to incorporate computers most effectively into instruction, and 3) software limitations that violate established pedagogical principles.[2]

We need to be reminded that many past technological innovations that were widely publicized as solutions to problems of teaching and learning simply failed to materialize. In a clever essay, Tyack and Hansot point out that "Those who seek pedagogical salvation in computers ignore the fate of earlier technological panaceas."[3] They go on to review such innovations as the blackboard (1841), radio, film, television, language laboratories, and programmed instruction. With the exception of the blackboard, which they say in retrospect has been "a modest triumph," all the others offered inflated promises, were poorly implemented, and never achieved their potential. They conclude that *teachers* remain the key to effective instruction, although their traditional roles may be modified by the computer. I agree that effective instruction resides in warm persons who care and who can communicate with learners of any age. For such persons the computer becomes a resource for extending human potential, not an electronic substitute for flashcards and workbook busywork.

Let us turn now to how able teachers can employ the computer to enhance the quality of living and learning in the microelectronic age.

Extending Human Potential with the Computer

Harvard psychologist Howard Gardner, in connection with his work on how children's thinking develops, has attracted a good deal of attention with his theory of multiple intelligences.[4] His thesis, of which able teachers long have been aware, is that people do not have a single intelligence. He has identified seven forms of intelligence.[5] Let us briefly examine Gardner's seven varieties of intelligence before we consider computers as curriculum resources in the next section. The two topics are intimately related!

Multiple intelligences. According to Gardner, the two forms of intelligence most highly valued by society are linguistic and logical-mathematical. Skills in these two realms are the ones commonly assessed on IQ tests. However, there are at least five other varieties of intelligence: 1) spatial, 2) musical, 3) bodily-kinesthetic, and two forms of "personal intelligence," 4) interpersonal and 5) intrapersonal. The former pertains to knowing how to interact effectively with others; the latter pertains to self-understanding.

Traditionally, American schools have stressed verbal and mathematical skills and, for the most part, have neglected or ignored the other five. However, in different times and in other cultures various combinations of the other intelligences have been prized and emphasized. In the apprenticeship era, which flourished before the industrial revolution, various body and spatial skills were highly desirable. In religious orders of yesteryear, musical, linguistic/memory, and interpersonal forms of intelligence were valued. In pre-agricultural hunting cultures, body control (kinesthetic) and knowing one's way around (spatial) probably were more valued than, say, mathematical ability.

Computers and multiple intelligences. Computers in the schools, if properly used, can nurture all varieties of intelligence. While the insight of teachers and the quality of teacher-pupil interaction will always be important, the computer also can personalize learning.

Computer problem solving can help fertilize logical-mathematical intelligence. Linguistic intelligence obviously is fostered by the computer since one of its inherent functions is as a communications device. Spatial knowledge, in the form of creating computer graphics, certainly can be enhanced. And a rich world of musical intelligence becomes available from databases currently available. Insofar as a bodily-kinesthetic intelligence is concerned, a case could be made that the manipulation of controls in playing various types of computer games develops hand-eye coordination.

If computers are to foster multiple intelligences of learners, the curriculum will have to be reinterpreted in terms of what the computer can do. This calls for new definitions of the curriculum.

Defining the Curriculum for Applications of the Computer

How educators define the curriculum ultimately will determine how computers will be used in the learning process. A brief review of how definitions of the curriculum have changed over the years provides historical perspective for understanding current computer applications.

Historical perspective. Until the 20th century the textbook largely determined what was taught.[6] The *New England Primer,* published in the 17th century, was steeped in religious content and was used by generations of Americans. Webster's spellers, first published in 1782, also became a mainstay of instruction. In various editions, more than a million copies were sold between 1840 and 1880. The *McGuffey Eclectic Readers,* first published in 1836, were concerned as much with imparting traditional morality as with teaching reading. They determined much of the content of what was learned in classrooms throughout the latter half of the 19th century and well into the 20th century. By 1920 an estimated 122 million copies of the readers had been purchased. Even after World War II, a 70,000 copy reprint edition was published and sold very well. Up to the present day, textbooks continue to determine much of what children learn. So, one definition of curriculum is the content of textbooks. But there are others.

A sampling of curriculum definitions. Over the years at least four distinct definitions of curriculum have evolved. Nearly 50 years ago Henry C. Morrison defined it as "the content of instruction without reference to instructional ways or means."[7] In the same vein, King and Brownell refer to the curriculum as "a planned series of encounters between a neophyte and the communities of symbolic discourse"[8] (that is, contact with the various disciplines). Definitions such as these would seem to restrict computer applications to drill or practice items and to conventional subject matter.

Appreciably different are some of the definitions coming out of the child-centered movement of the 1930s that define curriculum as "those experiences of the child which the school in any way utilizes or attempts to influence."[9] Here we find the school becoming more concerned with the whole child

71

rather than just with academic content. Greater attention to society's needs is reflected in a third definition by Smith, Stanley, and Shores: "a series of potential experiences . . . set up in school for the purpose of disciplining children and youth in group ways of thinking and acting."[10] The fourth, and perhaps most subtle, definition of curriculum is a psychological one that encompasses the sum total of "inner being" learnings that influence each student's behavior. As Harris puts it, "there will be as many curriculums as there are teachers and . . . children."[11] In effect, there is an *inner* curriculum for each learner.

A definition of curriculum for the microelectronic age. Each of the four definitions of curriculum has certain virtues; and all four, no doubt, could be braided into a strand of desirable curriculum practices. In my view, however, such definitions are inadequate for the microelectronic age. Therefore, I propose the following definition:

> The curriculum is a written document that outlines suggested learning experiences but also recognizes individual differences in a given age group.
>
> The curriculum reflects a consensus among faculty as to the scope and sequence of various learnings and includes ways of introducing learners to the values of a given culture. An effective curriculum results in desired changes in an individual's social, psychological, and intellectual behavior.

The curriculum needs to be in written form so that teachers can consult it and periodically make needed revisions. Also, it should specify certain vital learning experiences to be shared by all. To avoid overlapping or needless repetition of content, there should be faculty consensus when preparing curriculum documents. Finally, evaluation of the curriculum requires measures of the extent to which desirable changes are made in each learner's behavior.

The proposed definition encompasses both the *subject-centered* and the *learner-centered* approach to curriculum. In the lifelong curriculum of the microelectronic era, it is my opinion that the learner-centered approach will be more appropriate with young children, but as they mature increasing stress can be placed on intellectual skills and content.

Now let us turn to some of the potential contributions the computer can make to teaching and learning.

Contributions of the Computer to Curriculum and Instruction

Following is a list of some ways in which the computer, if used wisely, can facilitate instruction. The list is not comprehensive; rather, it is intended to suggest a few of many creative approaches a faculty might consider for a particular school.

1. Developing in learners a respect for the processes of inquiry, which can be broadened and accelerated by access to various computer databases.
2. Allowing teachers to provide for individual differences through the use of varied software selected in terms of students' maturity and level of competency.
3. Extending learning opportunities beyond the resources of the school through networking with students' home computers
4. Providing teachers with the means of making periodic assessments of individual academic achievement.
5. Challenging gifted children with a greater variety and quantity of electronic information input than traditional group instruction can provide.
6. Aiding slower learners with personalized experiences appropriate to their level of achievement, thus avoiding the pressure and frustration they experience from the demands of uniform classroom instruction.

As software improves and hardware becomes more versatile, learning is likely to become more self-directed. And a widening range of performance among learners can be anticipated. Another outcome is that the current segmented curriculum structure increasingly will become blurred as progress is made toward a seamless learning continuum. Further, the computer holds the potential of personalizing instruction in terms of learning styles. It follows that the testing and evaluation of knowledge and skills also will be more individualized. In the final analysis, the computer's major contribution is likely to be in helping us cope with the problems of mass education mentioned in Chapter 7.

Computers and the Learning Environment

If current trends continue, many schools in the 21st century will be structures designed using the principles of "architronics," a term used to describe the coordination of architectural design with electronic technology.[12]

The environment of such schools will be controlled by computers to maintain proper temperature and illumination, to monitor the status of locked or unlocked doors, and to alert staff to any fire or smoke in the building. Intraschool and interschool phone systems with visual screens will facilitate communication in larger districts, and long-distance calls will automatically shift to the most inexpensive circuitry available.[13] Even with all these technological innovations, no school can be operated as if it were a huge computerized teaching machine. We must remember that to date no computer has shown any interest in how it affects human beings. It takes people to create an enabling learning environment. Computers can lubricate and expedite teachers' work; they cannot take over the roles that only humans are qualified to fill.

The Computer and Curriculum Content

The computer obviously has many contributions to make to methods of instruction. It also has contributions to make to the content areas: communication skills, foreign languages, mathematics, science, the social studies, and other subject matter fields.

Communication skills. In an information society, a high premium is placed on communication skills — skills that will be taught differently with developments in word-processing programs. In 1985 Smith-Corona marketed a fully electronic portable typewriter that alerts one to spelling errors as one types! It has a computer that, according to the promotional literature, "instantaneously proofreads your typing against a dictionary of 50,000 most-used words. . . . Whenever you make a typo or spelling slip, it alerts you with a soft beep."[14] Even more remarkable is the development of such items as the Writer's Workbench™ program originally produced at Bell Laboratories to improve the writing of Bell engineers. By 1986 the program had reached a level of development where it "performs an exhaustive analysis of a writer's work — from grammar and punctuation errors to organization, weak phrasing, vague wording, even sexist usages."[15] By 1986 AT&T was selling a version of Writer's Workbench expressly designed for high school and college students. A number of large companies on the Fortune 500 list are contemplating using such programs for their staffs.

These developments raise an interesting paradox for the English classroom. Does the student or the computer receive the grade for a term paper? Will the computer make it easier not to learn to write good English? Or as technologist Michael Newman suggests, is it the ultimate destiny of the computer to make creative writing a mass phenomenon? Newman has devised a poetry word-processor program that automatically sets up the meter and stanza and suggests rhyming words with which to end lines.[16]

Beyond doubt the years ahead will be interesting ones for the teacher of communication skills if some of the current forecasts materialize. One can envision telling a story or making a statement to a computer and having its word processor ghostwrite a mellifluous, grammatically and syntactically perfect product!

74

Foreign languages. Because the information age links nations much more closely (verbally and visually) by satellites, a strong case can be made for learning a second language. We can no longer maintain the arrogant posture that other countries should learn English. We also should keep in mind Goethe's admonition that no one really understands one's own language until one has learned another. The computer has introduced new dimensions to foreign language instruction. For example, there is now a word-processor program that can help an American avoid errors when writing in, say, French, or can help a French speaker write correct English.[17] Also, for some time we have had electronic translation devices, which at present are used primarily as a novelty for tourists. They do not replace rigorous study of a second language.

Mathematics and science. The computer has many uses in mathematics and the sciences. But probably its most important use is to provide learners with the tools to validate data. As economist Leo Cherne has aptly stated:

> The computer is incredibly fast, accurate, and stupid. Man is unbelievably slow, inaccurate, and brilliant. The marriage of the two is a force beyond calculation.[18]

Students must be made aware of the need to validate carefully the data retrieved or produced by computers and hand calculators. Otherwise, they may find wrong answers with lightning speed. Students also must realize that computers cannot understand ambiguity in language. As Alson points out, "They [computers] never read between the lines while humans are able to, or do, just that."[19] He concludes that explicitness of meaning becomes increasingly important whenever computers are used for validating data in mathematics and science.

Social studies. The changing world that technology has created is the domain of the social studies. In addition to studying traditional content, learners at all levels need to understand humankind's problems. These include inner-city decay, hunger, the have and have-not gap, welfare costs, unemployment, population explosion, economic interdependence, energy deficits, air and water pollution, nuclear waste, terrorism, and arms control, to name a few.[20] An equally important role of the social studies is to foster mutual respect among peoples of the world, to develop an understanding of global economic interdependence, and to create an awareness of the need for viable supranational organizations concerned with health, disaster relief, and sharing the oceans' resources. It is through the social studies that students will learn about the world that microelectronic technology is creating. The social studies provide the knowledge enabling students to rethink the future and to work on solutions to the problems listed above.

Other curriculum areas. Art, music, vocational education, physical education, library skills, and special education are some of the other curriculum areas that are in some measure mediated by the computer. It offers graphics for art and a rich variety of input for music, including computer composition. In the library, Computer Assisted Reference Service (CARS) enables students to search 200 electronic databases for information. Special education services can be extended to the homebound via computer. Vocational education has a new role in preparing students with new skills for the changing workplace and for retraining displaced workers.

Concluding Comment

Much has been written on the need for curriculum change as we approach a millennium in which the computer will profoundly influence living and learning. My brief review of the issues has not been to offer prescriptions for educational change; rather, my intent has been to stress the need for constant and careful thought, imagination, and cooperatively developed innovations in ways our educational services are delivered.

An example of the challenges is a venture under way at the Massachusetts Institute of Technology, in cooperation with the Digital Equipment Corporation, called Project Athena. They are exploring the desirability of transposing undergraduate courses to telecommunication networks. The concept is exciting, because the students' computer screens could present many things that extend beyond the resources of a traditional classroom. In a decade or so, some comparable "electronic learning" might well be accessible for students at high schools or elementary schools.

The implicit challenge to readers of *Teaching and Learning in a Microelectronic Age* is to create schools that are relevant to our electronic surround, an environment with unlimited possibilities. The ultimate relevant education we should seek, in my opinion, is one that will allow us to continue living on a planet that is capable of maintaining a peaceful, clean, and comfortable support system for humanity.

Footnotes

1. "Computer Integration into Instruction Is Stuck," *Update* 27 (Summer 1985): 6-8.
2. A number of studies have pointed out that computers in the school have been used primarily for drill, practice, games, and other unimaginative activities.
3. David Tyack and Elizabeth Hansot, "Futures That Never Happened: Technology and the Classroom," *Education Week,* 4 September 1985, pp. 40, 35.
4. Howard Gardner, *Frames of Mind: The Theory of Multiple Intelligences* (New York: Basic Books, 1983).

5. For an interesting commentary, see "Human Intelligence Isn't What We Think It Is," *U.S. News and World Report,* 19 March 1984, pp. 75-76.

6. For a detailed and scholarly treatment of the topic, see *The Textbook in American Education,* 30th Yearbook of the National Society for the Study of Education, Part II (Bloomington, Ill.: Public School Publishing Company, 1931).

7. Henry C. Morrison, *The Curriculum of the Common School* (Chicago: University of Chicago Press, 1940), p. 58.

8. Arthur R. King and John A. Brownell, *The Curriculum and the Disciplines of Knowledge* (New York: John Wiley and Sons, 1966), p. 213.

9. Dorris Lee and Murray Lee, *The Child and His Curriculum* (New York: D. Appleton, 1940), p. 165.

10. B. Othanel Smith, W.O. Stanley, and J. Harlan Shores, *Fundamentals of Curriculum Development* (New York: World Book, 1950), p. 4.

11. P.E. Harris, *The Curriculum and Cultural Change* (New York: D. Appleton, 1937), p. 443.

12. For additional information on architronics, see Roy Mason, *The Computerized Home of Tomorrow* (Washington, D.C.: Acropolis Books, 1983).

13. The innovations noted here are already operational in such architronic marvels as the Lincoln Plaza office tower in downtown Dallas. See *Time,* June 1985, p. 77.

14. From a Smith Corona advertisement in the December 1985 catalogue, *The Sharper Image,* p. 30.

15. Michael Rogers, in the "Technology" section of *Newsweek,* 2 September 1985, p. 79.

16. Ibid.

17. Ibid.

18. Cited in the *Christian Science Monitor,* 1981 reprint, "Computers: The New Industrial Revolution," p. 1.

19. David R. Alson, "Computers as Tools of the Intellect," *Educational Researcher* 14 (May 1985): 7.

20. For an excellent annual summary of world conditions and problems, see Lester R. Brown et al., *State of the World* (New York: W.W. Norton & Company).

Epilogue

The implicit message in the eight chapters of *Teaching and Learning in a Microelectronic Age* is that learners at any age, but especially educators, need to be informed about the technology and world conditions that are likely to affect the future. It is crucial that we do both short- and long-range planning – planning based on available data and perceived trends. Furthermore, we must engage in reasoned speculation with regard to what lies over the horizon in the next three decades. Failure to do so could find us unprepared to cope with a rapidly changing environment. We need to develop in all learners the quality that I call "educated foresight," the attainment of which will enable us to create policies for a humane future.

Appendix
Digests of Education Reform Reports

Digests of the recommendations from 18 of the major education reform reports released in the 1980s are presented below. For a more complete summary of virtually all the reform reports, see: Beatrice Gross and Ronald Gross, eds., *The Great School Debate: Which Way for American Education?* (New York: Simon and Schuster, 1985).

1. *A Nation At Risk* initiated a national discussion on education reform. More rigorous standards for students are reflected in recommendations for a longer school day and school year; a core curriculum consisting of English, mathematics, science, social studies, and computer science; and close monitoring of student achievement. More rigorous standards for teachers are implicit in the recommendations for career ladders, market-sensitive salaries, and scholarships for outstanding teacher candidates. (National Commission on Excellence in Education 1983)

2. *Action for Excellence* highlights the state's role in improving education. This role encompasses strengthening the curriculum; intensifying learning; monitoring student achievement; raising standards for teacher certification, recruitment, and evaluation; and utilizing qualified persons outside of education to serve in the nation's schools. (Education Commission of the States 1983)

3. *Educating Americans for the 21st Century* is a renewed demand to intensify math, science, and technology instruction in America's schools. To implement these demands school systems should consider lengthening the school day and year. The report also echoes the demand for rigorous promotion and graduation standards. (The National Science Board, Commission on Precollege Education in Mathematics, Science, and Technology 1983)

4. *America's Competitive Challenge: The Need for a National Response* reiterates the emphasis on math, science, and technology. The report also calls on industry to support reform and research. (Business-Higher Education Forum 1983)

5. *Federal Elementary and Secondary Education Policy* explicates the roles of local, state, and federal governments in education reform that supports the nation's competitive economy. Core components of the curriculum should encompass reading, writing, calculating, computer skills, science, foreign language, and civics, with the overriding objective being literacy in English. (The Twentieth Century Fund Task Force 1983)

6. *Academic Preparation for College: What Students Need to Know and Be Able to Do* highlights appropriate collegiate preparation. Such preparation should include the intellectual skills of reading, writing, speaking and listening, mathematics, reasoning, and studying. Preparation should also include the arts, sciences, and computer knowledge. (The College Board 1983)

7. *A Study of Schooling* suggests age 4 as the ideal age for youngsters to begin school. The report recommends replacing grades with phases, eliminating junior highs and tracking schemes, establishing curriculum centers, organizing teacher teams to deliver instruction, and developing potential leaders to serve as principals. (John I. Goodlad, *A Place Called School.* New York: McGraw-Hill, 1984)

8. *High School: A Report On Secondary Schooling In America* introduces the New Carnegie Unit to stimulate students' community involvement, stresses the teaching of writing, and recommends a global core curriculum to enhance student understanding of the world's interdependence. Suggestions to enhance working conditions for teachers and to rectify the problems of school dropouts are detailed. (The Carnegie Foundation for the Advancement of Teaching 1983)

9. *Information Technology and Its Impact on American Education* was commissioned by the U.S. House of Representatives and carried out by its Subcommittees on Special Education and on Science, Research, and Technology and compiled by the Office of Technology Assessment. It concluded that the information revolution is changing what needs to be learned, who needs to learn it, who will provide it, and how it will be provided and paid for. New technology can improve education services that traditional institutions provide, can distribute education to new places such as the home and office, can reach new clients such as the handicapped and homebound, and can teach job-related skills in the use of technology. (Office of Technology Assessment 1983)

10. *Making the Grade* addresses the school's role in serving the poor, the handicapped, and non-English-speaking peoples. The federal government is called on to provide financial resources to upgrade the schooling of these groups. (Twentieth Century Fund Task Force on Federal Elementary and Secondary Education 1983)

11. *The Failure of Our Public Schools: The Causes and a Solution* explicates in greater depth those facts revealed in *A Nation at Risk.* (National Center for Policy Analysis, University of Dallas 1983)

12. *The National Science Foundation Report* underscores declining student achievement in math and science and the failure of the schools to integrate math, science, and technology. Calls on the schools to raise the math, science, and technology literacy of all citizens. (National Science Foundation 1983)

13. *Paideia Problems and Possibilities: A Consideration of Questions Raised by the Paideia Proposal* responds to questions raised by parents and educators regarding *The Paideia Proposal,* which would require all students to undertake a uniform course of study throughout their 12 years of schooling. Discusses the value of extracurricular activities, the impact of eliminating electives, the role of vocational schools, the ideal teacher-student ratio for Socratic teaching, and the role of technology and computer literacy. (Prepared on behalf of the Paideia Group by Mortimer J. Adler. New York: Macmillan Publishing Company, 1983)

14. *A Nation Prepared: Teachers for the 21st Century* makes seven major recommendations: 1) establishing a national board for professional teaching standards, 2) using "lead teachers" to help colleagues maintain desired standards, 3) requiring a bachelor's degree in the arts and sciences as a prerequisite to the professional study of education, 4) allowing teachers to decide how best to meet professional goals but holding them accountable for pupil progress, 5) increasing the preparation of minorities to enter teaching, 6) providing technological resources to improve teacher productivity, and 7) making teachers' salaries competitive with other professions. (Carnegie Task Force on Teaching as a Profession 1986)

15. *Transforming American Education: Reducing the Risk to the Nation* explores broad, sound uses of technology. Recommended reading for persons interested in the fundamental redesign of U.S. education, this report examines the changing role of the school resulting from the new information technology. It calls for redesigning education to take into account the impact of microelectronic technology. (U.S. Department of Education 1986)

81

16. *Transforming the State Role in Undergraduate Education* stresses the need for universities to create a better balance between narrow career training and general education and the need for secondary schools to ensure that students acquire the basic skills necessary for success in higher education. (Education Commission of the States 1986)

17. *Tomorrow's Teachers: A Report of the Holmes Group*, generated by a team of deans of schools of education, makes five recommendations to improve teaching and teacher education: 1) more rigorous education of teachers in the liberal arts, subject matter of their teaching field, literature of education, and reflective practical experience; 2) a multi-level career structure that recognizes differences in knowledge, skill, and commitment among teachers; 3) multiple evaluations of preservice students before issuing teaching certificates; 4) professional development schools that are analogous to the medical profession's teaching hospitals; and 5) improved working conditions for teachers. (Holmes Group 1986)

18. *Ventures in Good Schooling: A Cooperative Model for a Successful Secondary School* is a carefully reasoned report on the need for 1) more cooperative principal-teacher relationships, 2) increasing instructional input, 3) evaluation and counseling to improve teacher performance, and 4) developing a strong sense of teacher-principal interdependence and community. It also calls for better linkages between school and community to ensure good student behavior and performance. (National Education Association, National Association of Secondary School Principals 1986)

Bibliography for the Microelectronic Age

Abrams, Floyd. "The New Effort to Control Information." *New York Times Magazine*, 25 September 1983, pp. 22-27.

Aleksander, Igor, and Burnett, Piers. *Reinventing Man: The Robot Becomes Reality.* New York: Holt, Rinehart & Winston, 1984.

Asimov, Isaac, ed. *Living in the Future.* New York: Beaufort, 1985.

Association for Supervision and Curriculum Development. "Preparing for the Future." *Educational Leadership* 41 (September 1983): 4-57.

Avery, Russell, ed. "From Drill Sargeant to Intellectual Assistant: Computers in the Schools." *Carnegie Quarterly* 30 (Summer-Fall 1985): 1-7.

Beaird, Richard C. "Communications: Commerce and Culture." *Information Society Journal* 1 (1982): 281-305.

Bennett, William J. *First Lessons: A Report on Elementary Education in America.* Washington, D.C.: U.S. Government Printing Office, 1986.

Blankenship, Jane, and Kenner, Janette. "Images of Tomorrow: How Advertisers Sell the Future." *The Futurist* 20 (May-June 1986): 19-20.

Bolter, J. David. *Turing's Man: Western Culture in the Computer Age.* Chapel Hill: University of North Carolina Press, 1984.

Boraiko, A. "The Chip." *National Geographic* 162 (October 1982): 421-57.

Boulding, Kenneth E. *The World as a Total System.* Beverly Hills, Calif.: Sage, 1985.

Boulding, Kenneth E., and Senesh, Lawrence, eds. *The Optimum Utilization of Knowledge: Making Knowledge Serve Human Betterment.* Academy of Independent Scholars Forum Series. Boulder, Colo.: Westview, 1983.

Bozeman, William C. *Computers and Computing in Education: An Introduction.* Scottsdale, Ariz.: Gorsuch Scarisbrick, 1985.

Brandt, Ronald. "On Reading, Writing, and Computers: A Conversation with John Henry Martin." *Educational Leadership* 39 (October 1981): 60-64.

Broad, W., and Wade, N. "Betrayers of the Truthe." *TWA Ambassador* (December 1982): 39-50.

Brophy, Beth. "New Technology, High Anxiety: Using Computers to Measure Productivity Can Backfire." *U.S. News and World Report*, 29 September 1986, pp. 54-55.

Brown, Lester R., et al. *State of the World 1986.* New York: W.W. Norton, 1986.

Campbell, Patricia F., ed. *Young Children and Microcomputers.* Englewood Cliffs, N.J.: Prentice-Hall, 1986.

Cassata, Mary, and Skill, Thomas. *Television: A Guide to the Literature.* Phoenix, Ariz.: Oryx, 1985.

Clarke, Arthur C. *Profiles of the Future: An Inquiry into the Limits of the Possible.* New York: Holt, Rinehart & Winston, 1984.

Committee on Science, Engineering, and Public Policy; National Academy of Sciences; National Academy of Engineering; and Institute of Medicine. *Frontiers in Science and Technology: A Selected Outlook.* San Francisco: W.H. Freeman, 1983.

"A Computer Training Center for the Visually Impaired." *Perspectives in Computing* 2 (October 1982): 49.

Corn, Joseph J., ed. *Imagining Tomorrow: History, Technology, and the American Future.* Cambridge, Mass.: MIT Press, 1986.

Daneshmend, T.K., and Campbell, M.J. "Dark Warrior Epilepsy." *British Medical Journal* 284 (June 1982): 1751-52.

Deken, Joseph. *The Electronic Cottage.* New York: William Morrow, 1982.

Didsbury, Howard F., Jr., ed. *Challenges and Opportunities from Now to 2001.* Bethesda, Md.: World Future Society, 1986.

Dunn, Samuel L. "The Changing University: Survival in the Information Society." *The Futurist* 17 (August 1983): 55-60.

Evans, Christopher. *The Micromillennium.* New York: Washington Square Press, 1979.

Finneran, Kevin. "The Future of the English Language." *The Futurist* 20 (July-August 1986): 9-13.

Friedman, Robert. "Supernews: Journalism in the High-Tech Mode." *Channels of Communication* 3 (September-October 1983): 26-30.

Gomes, L. "Secrets of the Software Pirates." *Esquire* (January 1982): 58-65.

Goodlad, John I. *A Place Called School: Prospects for the Future.* New York: McGraw-Hill, 1984.

Grady, Tim M., and Gawronski, Jane D., eds. *Computers in Curriculum and Instruction.* Alexandria, Va.: Association for Supervision and Curriculum Development, 1983.

Greenberg, Daniel. "High-Tech America's Myopic Mind-Set." *Time*, 22 September 1986, pp. 64-65.

Hearst, D. "Computer Age Will Be Costly for Schools." *Times* (London), 15 December 1982, p. 22.

Hodgkinson, Harold L. "What's Ahead for Education." *Principal* (January 1986): 6-11.

Holusha, John. "Electronic 'Pollution' Plays Havoc with Modern Devices." *New York Times,* 20 December 1983. p. 58.

Hubbard, Guy. "Computer Graphics as an Art Form for Schools." *Printout* 2 (November 1985): 3-4.

Hudson, Heather. *Telecommunications and Development.* Norwood, N.J.: Ablex, 1983.

Huntley, S. "Keyboard Bandits Who Steal Money." *U.S. News and World Report,* 27 December 1982, 3 January 1983, pp. 68-69.

84

Jackson, Kenneth T. *Crabgrass Frontier: The Suburbanization of the United States.* New York: Oxford University Press, 1985.

Johnston, M. "Silicon Valley." *National Geographic* (October 1982): 459-77.

Kanfer, Stefan. "Heard Any Good Books Lately? Literature on Cassettes Is a Best Selling Business." *Time,* 21 July 1986, pp. 71-72.

Klapp, Orin E. *Overload and Boredom: Essays on the Quality of Life in the Information Society.* Westport, Conn.: Greenwood Press, 1986.

Koepp, Steven. "And Now the Age of Light," *Time,* 6 October 1986, p. 56.

Kupisiewicz, Czeslaw. "School and the Mass Media." *Prospects* 14 (1984): 11-21.

Larick, Keith T., Jr., and Fischer, Jock. "Classrooms of the Future: Introducing Technology to Schools." *The Futurist* 22 (May-June 1986): 21-22.

"A Library on a Disc: CD's Go Beyond Music." *Newsweek,* 21 April 1986, p. 73.

Lockheed, Marlaine E., and Mandinach, Ellen B. "Trends in Educational Computing: Decreasing Interest and the Changing Focus of Instruction." *Educational Researcher* 15 (May 1986): 21-26.

McHale, Magda Cordell, and Harris, David A. "Three Views of the Information Revolution." *World Future Society Bulletin* 17 (May-June 1983): 19-22.

McKeown, Patrick G. *Living with Computers.* San Diego: Harcourt Brace Jovanovich, 1986.

McLaughlin, William I. "Human Evolution in the Age of the Intelligent Machine." *Interdisciplinary Science Reviews* 8 (December 1983): 307-19.

Malik, Rex. "Beyond the Exponential Cascade: On the Reduction of Complexity." *InterMedia* 14 (March 1986): 14-31.

Marien, Michael, ed. "Some Questions for the Information Society." *World Future Society Bulletin* 17 (September-October 1983): 17-23.

Mecklenburger, James A. "Looking Back to School." *Phi Delta Kappan* 67 (October 1985): 119-22.

Olson, David R. "Computers as Tools of the Intellect." *Educational Researcher* 14 (May 1985): 5-8.

Otway, Harry J., and Peltu, Malcolm, eds. *New Office Technology: Human and Organizational Aspects.* Norwood, N.J.: Ablex, 1983.

Perelman, Lewis J. "Learning Our Lesson: Why School Is Out." *The Futurist* 22 (March-April 1986): 13-16.

Pierce, Jean. "Computer Network." *Educational Researcher* 14 (December 1985): 21-22.

Pogrow, Stanley. *Education in the Computer Age: Issues of Policy, Practice, and Reform.* Beverly Hills, Calif.: Sage, 1983.

Postel, Sandra. *Altering the Earth's Chemistry: Assessing the Risks.* Washington, D.C.: Worldwatch Institute, 1986.

Ranney, Austin. *Channels of Power: The Impact of Television on American Politics.* New York: Basic Books, 1983.

Ravitch, Diane. "On Thinking About the Future." *Phi Delta Kappan* 64 (January 1983): 317-20.

Reinhold, Robert. "Machines Built to Emulate Human Experts' Reasoning." *New York Times,* 29 March 1984, p. 1.

Ridley, William J., et al. "Transforming American Education: Reducing the Risk to the Nation." *School Board News,* 25 June 1986, pp. 8-12.

Rivlin, R. "Computer Graphics." *Omni* (November 1982): 32-35.

Roszak, Theodore. *The Cult of Information: The Folklore of Computers and the True Art of Thinking.* New York: Pantheon, 1986.

Rubinstein, Ellis, ed. "Beyond 1984: Technology and the Individual." *IEEE Spectrum* 21 (June 1984): 26-135.

Salamon, Michael. *Future Life.* Trans. Guy Daniels. New York: Macmillan, 1983.

Seif, Elliot. "The Need for Futures Thinking." *World Future Society Bulletin* 17 (March-April 1983): 8-12.

Shane, Harold G. *The Educational Significance of the Future.* Bloomington, Ind.: Phi Delta Kappa Educational Foundation, 1973.

Shane, Harold G., and Tabler, M. Bernadine. *Educating for a New Millennium.* Bloomington, Ind.: Phi Delta Kappa Educational Foundation, 1981.

Siegal, Martin A. *Understanding Computer-Based Education.* New York: Random House, 1986.

Skinner, B.F. "Programmed Instruction Revisited." *Phi Delta Kappan* 68 (October 1986): 103-10.

"Software: The New Driving Force." *Business Week,* 27 February 1984, pp. 74-98.

Solozano, Lucia, et al. "Teaching in Trouble." *U.S. News and World Report,* 26 May 1986, pp. 52-57.

Stewart, David; Keegan, Desmond; and Holmberg, Borje, eds. *Distance Education: International Perspectives.* New York: St. Martin's Press, 1983.

Sweeney, Gerry, ed. "Information Technology and Development." *Information Society Journal* 2, no. 1 (1983): 1-89.

Sylvester, Edward J., and Klotz, Lynn C. *The Gene Age: Genetic Engineering and the New Industrial Revolution.* New York: Charles Scribner's Sons, 1983.

Tanakadate, H. " 'Science City,' Japan's New Challenge to U.S." *U.S. News and World Report,* 10 January 1983, p. 40.

Taylor, Robert P., ed. *The Computer in the School: Tutor, Tool, Tutee.* New York: Teachers College Press, 1980.

Time-Life Books. *Understanding Computers.* Series introduced in August 1986. Alexandria, Va.

Torrero, Edward A., ed. "Tomorrow's Computers." *IEEE Spectrum* 20 (November 1983): 34-120.

"University Computer 'Cracked'." *The Scotsman,* 23 December 1982, p. 5.

U.S. Office of Technology Assessment. *Electronic Record Systems and Individual Privacy.* Washington, D.C.: U.S. Government Printing Office, 1986.

Wakefield, Rowan A. "Home Computers and Families." *The Futurist* 20 (September-October 1986): 18-22.

Walker, Decker F. "Reflections on the Educational Potential and Limitations of Microcomputers." *Phi Delta Kappan* 65 (October 1983): 103-107.

Weiner, Edith, and Brown, Arnold. "Issues for the 1990's." *The Futurist* 20 (March-April 1986): 9-12.

Weisman, John. "Network News: Are We Better Informed Now — Or Worse?" *TV Guide,* 23 August 1986, pp. 6-10.

Yoxen, Edward. *The Gene Business: Who Should Control Biotechnology.* New York: Harper & Row, 1984.